FIVE STAR FOOD

THE VANCOUVER SUN

Also by Eve Johnson: *Six O'Clock Solutions*

First printing: September 1993.
Second printing: November 1993.
Third printing: February 1999.

Published by
Pacific Press, Division of Southam Inc.
1 – 200 Granville Street
Vancouver, B.C.
V6C 3N3

Southam President and C.O.O.: Donald Babick

Canadian Cataloguing in Publication Data
Johnson, Eve
Five star food
Includes Index.
ISBN 0-9697356-0-X
1. Cookery. I. Vancouver Sun (Firm). II. Title.
TX714.J63 1993 641.5 C93-091586-0

Design: Blair Pocock, Fleming Design Group
Cover design: Dan Murray
Illustrations: Michael Knox
Photography: Peter Battistoni (front cover)
Bill Keay (back cover)
Home economist: Brenda Thompson
Index: Jan Wallace
Editor: Daphne Gray-Grant

Printed and bound in Canada

Cover plates: Top: Block Molde "Apples"
2nd: Worcester "Herbs"
(courtesy Kim-John China & Gifts)
3rd: Sasaki "Pompeii"
4th: Limoges Puiforcat "Les Nacres"
(courtesy Atkinson's);
chocolate and strawberry sauce
painted by Brenda Thompson

Distributed by: Whitecap Books
361 Lynn Avenue
North Vancouver, B.C. V7J 2C4

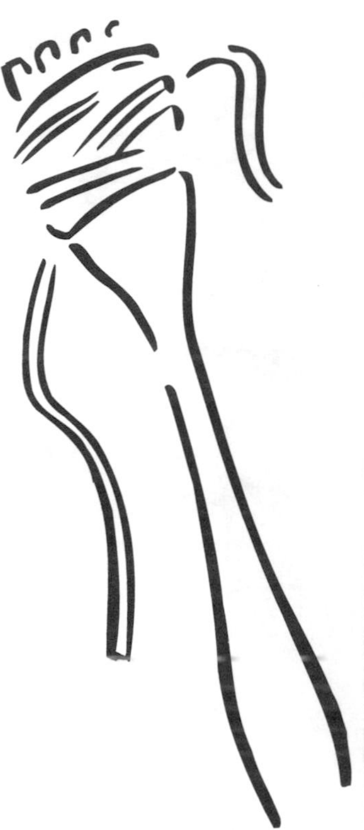

THIRD PRINTING PREFACE

Apart from this preface and a few additions to the cover — including a shiny gold "Canadian Best-Seller" sticker — only one change distinguishes this edition of Five-Star Food *from the first two.*

Pear Upside-Down Gingerbread (p.45) now calls for "small pears," instead of just "pears," an improvement which should spare Brenda Thompson, the home economist responsible for making these recipes clear and accurate, her recurring nightmare that some ill-fated cook will use very large pears and the cake will overflow in the oven.

Brenda's awe-inspiring capacity to see traps for the unwary in what looks like an otherwise harmless recipe is one of the reasons Five-Star Food *has been such an overwhelming success. After the first two printings sold out, we still had requests for it, most often from people who loved the book and wanted more copies for gifts, or who wanted, as a friend told me, to get out of "always photocopying recipes for people."*

Why is Five-Star Food *so popular? The historian in me wants to believe it's because the "modest but true picture of home cooking on Canada's West Coast" we drew six years ago remains the only attempt so far to explain how we came to eat the way we do.*

Reality suggests something simpler: Five-Star Food *is a reliable source of excellent recipes with an emphasis on food for special occasions. There are those who would argue that Ocean Park caterer Jane Bailey's Chocolate-Dipped Cappuccino Shortbread (p.147), versions of which are becoming a holiday staple in some Vancouver bakeries, are worth the price of admission. Others might nominate Coquitlam firefighter David Veljacic's Barbecued Salmon with Sun-Dried Tomatoes (p.18) as the recipe that's become the most treasured addition to the good tastes of home.*

Since Five-Star Food *was first printed, we've learned that the recipe for Chocolate Bar Chocolate Chip Cookies (p.140) is the same as the one often circulated as the Neiman Marcus cookie. Under that name it comes complete with an urban legend: a customer, charged $250 for the recipe and refused a refund, is now bent on revenge and wants the recipe circulated as widely as possible. This story persists, despite repeated denials on the part of the department store, which has never sold a recipe to a customer nor served a chocolate chip recipe in its restaurant. Bogus story or not, it's a good cookie.*

Anyone who writes a cookbook incurs debts of gratitude to dozens of people. My list is particularly long. It begins with all of the cooks who have tested recipes in the Vancouver Sun test kitchen over the past 50 years. Their dedication to accuracy and clarity established our reputation for recipes that work.

Special thanks go to Barbara McQuade, food editor for all but one year of the period covered by this cookbook. Her tastes are reflected in many of the recipes.

The cooks and home economists who tested recipes for this book are Pat Pederson, Brenda Thompson, Yvette Stachowiak, Ruth Phelan and Darlene Thompson.

Until Pat Pederson retired in 1992, Pat and Brenda were the core kitchen crew. You'll feel Pat's influence throughout this cookbook — especially in its down-to-earth practicality.

We've also profited from the generosity of chefs and readers. A warm thanks goes to Stephen Wong, whose Pacific Rim column brought a new level of culinary understanding to the kitchen, the newspaper and this book.

Thanks go to marketing manager Susan Semeniw; Steve Proulx, Debbie Millward and the Press Library staff; Craig Ferry and Wayne Smith of editorial systems; Tom Hemmy and his photo department colleagues; Jenafor Shaffer in the executive office; Carole Bridge and Gordon Hood in accounting; Marilyn Chepil at the promotions desk; and Vanessa Pinniger, who helped in the tedious work of proofreading. Murray McMillan, a regular taste-tester and our favorite dial-a-curmudgeon, provided grammatical advice on demand (any errors remaining are not his fault).

Deputy managing editor Shelley Fralic and then life-section editor Karenn Krangle both lent their keen support to this book. The design team at Fleming Design Group made this book easy to read and good to look at, and handled the changes for this printing. Michael Knox provided the charming illustrations; Dan Murray designed the cover.

This book wouldn't exist without the support of Southam president and Pacific Press publisher Don Babick. His belief in the project helped make it a reality. Southam Newspaper Group VP Dennis Skulsky gave the nod to this third printing.

Editor Daphne Gray-Grant remains as ever, this book's organizational angel. Six years ago I called her "razor-sharp, persistent, inventive, good humored and always able to improve my copy." It's all still true, only more so.

Finally, thanks go to Alan, for his unfailing love and support.

Eve Johnson
Vancouver, B.C.
February, 1999

★ ★ ★ ★ ★

Contents

★

★ ★ ★ ★ ★

On the Rim

Ciao Italian Style

Chocolate

Reflections on a Kitchen, A Cookbook and a Newspaper

The book you hold in your hands is the logical product of an illogical fact: there is a fully operating kitchen in the building where The Vancouver Sun is printed.

Newspapers do not, strictly speaking, need kitchens. Newspapers produce news stories, photographs, analysis and illustrations. Their business is more often with the serious events in the world. Editors don't lean back in their chairs and bellow: "Get me that blueberry muffin recipe right away!" and they never did. I've worked 15 years in this troubled industry, and I have yet to see a high-priced media consultant give a worried publisher a report that says: "Put a kitchen in here or you're sunk."

Nonetheless, since 1947, The Vancouver Sun has believed strongly enough in the importance of food to operate a test kitchen. Week after week, year after year, this newspaper puts its commitment to accuracy on the kitchen counter.

What is Five-Star Food?

In The Vancouver Sun's food section, we don't print recipes we haven't tested for ourselves. We use home equipment and locally available ingredients. Then we ask a panel of outspoken, not to say cheeky, tasters what they think.

With three or four exceptions, our tasters – the editors, reporters, graphic artists and secretaries we regularly call to the kitchen – are not epicures. Food enthusiasts more than foodies, they are all capable of the terrible honesty every cook craves and dreads at the same time.

We tape a tasting sheet to the kitchen cupboard and anyone who eats the food also rates it: excellent, good or fair. There are times when we are asked if "truly awful" couldn't be added as category. There are other times when a recipe earns raves – not just check marks but stars and exclamation points – and those we call five-star recipes.

The recipes in this book have been tasted and rated superb, each in its own way. It's true this rating system is skewed towards drama. Depending on the taster, certain foods – chocolate desserts, or prime rib roasts, or anything with balsamic vinegar in it – start with four stars and can only go up. Vegetables usually have to try harder (which is one reason the vegetable recipes are some of the best in this book).

Once you have a kitchen in the newspaper, churning out tested recipes every week, it's only logical to publish a cookbook. So the quick response to the question "What is Five-Star Food?" is this: It is a collection of the best recipes printed in The Vancouver Sun food pages in the eight years since Barbara McQuade's enormously popular Five-Star Recipes.

But the short answer doesn't tell you what makes these recipes special. It doesn't tell you why readers have been asking for a new cookbook, or why the first 10,000 copies of Barbara's book sold out in two weeks. To understand what Five-Star Food is really about, you need the long answer, and that means a trip into the past.

Illustrations on pages 5, 6 and 9 from Edith Adams promotional materials of the '30s, '40s and '50s

THE TRUTH ABOUT EDITH ADAMS

If you read The Sun's food pages, you've probably noticed the column Edith Adams Answers. If you're over 35, you will remember a time when Edith's personality suffused every Wednesday's paper. But here is the harsh truth: There is no Edith Adams. There never was one. There was only, back in 1912, a Mr. Gates. The written record says he was an editor. Rumor has it he was a typesetter. In either case, he thought the name looked good across a column of type – no descenders. So he made her up, just like Betty Crocker, except Edith never sat for a portrait.

We do not know the day Edith Adams's name first appeared in the newspaper – although we assume some time in 1912. By 1927, she was stick-handling a daily feature called Readers' Favorite Recipes. Readers sent in their recipes, home economists at the B.C. Electric Company (now B.C. Hydro) tested them, and The Sun ran one every day, awarding its author a dollar in prize money.

Edith, or whoever was currently operating under her mantle, also organized cooking schools. On three afternoons in May, 1937, for example, The Vancouver Sun sponsored Miss Claire Andree, instructress at the DeBoth Homemakers' School, at the Orpheum, and reported that Miss Andree demonstrated a number of dishes – mincemeat ice cream, minced bologna sandwiches, fish-stuffed pepper cases and "macaroni orientale" – to a crowded house. It's easy enough to smile indulgently at Miss Andree's culinary offering, and at her audience, who paid 25 cents a head and appear to have been grievously overcharged. But Miss Andree also cooked broccoli, and we can assume by the reporter's description – "a vegetable easily obtained here in season, but which until recently has been comparatively little used" – that much of her audience had just clapped eyes on a new food.

Ten years later, women found themselves in an entirely new world. The war was over, but the home front had become more complex. In B.C., homemakers could turn to several services. The Province newspaper had a staff of home economists who tested recipes and answered questions over the phone. Woodward's and Simpson Sears department stores kept home economists on staff to answer questions concerning food and major appliances. B.C. Electric's home economists made house calls to demonstrate the care and use of equipment, and would even plan kitchens for customers.

But Edith Adams stood out above them all. In 1947, she opened the doors to her "cottage," a suite of rooms, with a private entrance at 510 Beatty Street. Edith could advise you on etiquette, show you how to make a cake or teach you to crochet. You could phone or drop in at any time during regular office hours.

A brochure from 1947 shows an artist's idea of Edith: an elderly woman at the door of her modest home, waving to a young woman who stands on Edith's garden path, coming to tea, or perhaps going home, armed with a new recipe for bread pudding and a strategy for getting ink spots out of rugs. In truth, by 1948, there were five women answering to "Edith Adams," four of them with home economics degrees. The best-known, Marianne Linnell, was 32 in 1947, widow of an RCAF squadron leader killed in action over Berlin, and mother of one son. A home economics graduate from the University of Alberta, she spent 10 years in the Cottage before founding a real estate company and, three years later, running successfully for city council.

Not being a real person didn't hamper Edith, any more than it did Betty Crocker; she was a living force to many of our readers. In the days when we still answered the phone as Edith Adams, this could lead to surreal conversations. On those occasions when the phone rang an especially long time, more than one caller said: "Oh, I hope I didn't get you out of the garden."

Until 1979, when Barbara McQuade became the first Sun food editor to write under her own byline, Edith Adams was the city's voice of homemaking authority. This is a proud tradition, especially in the Lower Mainland, where anything that survives from 1912 is rare indeed. But here is the second, harder truth about Edith Adams: we no longer share her approach to food. Edith is not just the past, she's the past we've grown beyond.

THE DAILY MIRROR

When you stop to think of it, of course, it couldn't be otherwise. A newspaper is tied directly to its readers; it lasts by appealing to their tastes. When you look at a newspaper, you can see its readers, just as they see themselves: in a jagged piece of the daily mirror. Pick up this partial reflection of a social order on any day and you will find scattered bits of all our obsessions: Ann Landers, news of a contract killing, a horoscope, war in Bosnia, poverty in Canada, an interview with Tina Turner and a story about an escaped alligator owned by a man who rents exotic animals to the movie industry, headlined: "Alligator gets recaptured after losing bid to quit movie career."

As we change, the paper changes. Still, when I look back at Edith Adams's food tastes, they strike me as nothing short of bizarre.

In December, 1947, at the end of the Cottage's first year, the newspaper ran a recipe contest seeking the best B.C. recipes. The contest announcement boldly asserted: "Somewhere in British Columbia there's a 'native dish' that, if widely adopted, could make this province famous the world over for its cooking," and encouraged cooks to send their recipes to Edith Adams, for a chance at $500 in prizes. The grand prize winner was a salmon, stuffed with oysters, larded with bacon and baked at 400 degrees F for 25 minutes a pound.

A recipe Edith particularly liked ("it deserves a special award") was Vancouver Island Salad: grated cabbage, apple, carrot, celery, sprinkled with icing sugar, mixed with a cup of whipping cream, moulded, turned out on to lettuce cups, decorated with banana slices, more whipped cream, maraschino cherries, and slices of cream-cheese-and-nut stuffed celery.

"No meal is complete without a vitamin-and-mineral-rich salad," Edith wrote in her comments. Cabbage, it turns out, had been the most often used salad ingredient in the contest entries. "Trimmed and decorated as in this attractive Vancouver Island Salad, it really raises the humble vegetable to the plane of the more exotic." Or, if you prefer, to the plane of the purely lunatic.

How could we ever, in our right minds, have suggested this? Turns out it was easy. Vancouver was a frontier town with a passion for the new. The new cookery, a continent-wide craze for home economics, for the baby science of nutrition and for manufactured food in packages from the supermarket, emphasized an odd set of principles, none of which had much to do with taste. We hadn't learned to distrust processed food; the flavor of chemicals was thrilling, not disturbing.

Food, naturally, isn't the only thing that's changed since 1947. On the front page of the paper the day the prize-winning recipes were printed we used the word "Jap" twice in headlines. In other front page news, a man had assaulted a woman on the street, striking her as she walked by. Police were investigating. A yellowed clipping from my mother's recipe file box gives a recipe for Broken Glass Dessert made with whipping cream, gelatin and three colors of jelly, cut into cubes. (Edith's comment: "This picture-pretty dessert is a wonderful conversation piece.")

Edith Adams adapted over the years, learning new techniques and coping with unfamiliar ingredients, but her personality and her love of packaged food stayed the same. She was a food authority, with the right answer to any homemaking dilemma, and the answer often lay in making sauce from a can of soup.

Changing Times

I suspect Edith stopped being an accurate reflection of Vancouver's home cooks some time around 1980. Immigration had already infused new life into Chinatown; Asian restaurants suddenly bloomed, in number and in quality. And in 1980, Granville Island Market opened, a cultural revolution in fresh food.

By the '80s, Edith Adams Cottage was in the midst of a sea change. The opportunity for color photography on the section-front gave us drama, but the food section itself had shrunk. In the past, when supermarkets advertised in the pages, we'd had sections 20 pages long. When, as they did all across North America, grocery chains began to use flyers instead, there were no food advertisements to wrap the recipes around. Our sections were four pages, sometimes six, seldom more. Without the advertising revenue, we could no longer afford to keep enough home economists on staff to answer the telephone.

But while Edith's influence faded, the kitchen stubbornly remained. Today, we still mail out recipes on request – and on receipt of a stamped, self-addressed envelope – as many as 60 a week before Christmas and during canning season. We still get our recipes from a multitude of sources, including, reliably, our readers. You'll find nine readers' recipes in this book. Other recipes come from growers' groups like the California Prune Advisory Board and from food companies. They come from magazines and cookbooks; unless we radically change the recipe, we credit the source. Increasingly, our recipes come from chefs who bring their ideas to the test kitchen where they cook under the watchful eye of home economist Brenda Thompson.

A WORD ABOUT THE ORGANIZATION OF THIS BOOK

I didn't expect this cookbook to be an exercise in self-revelation. It was, primarily, a response to requests, driven by the nature of clippings. Clipped recipes disappear into obscure cookbooks, drift to the backs of drawers and vanish, treacherously, at the worst possible moment. We wanted to give our readers one book in which we hoped they'd find their favorite recipes.

Editor Daphne Gray-Grant and I sat down to wrestle a coherent book from a pile of 400 five-star recipes. We read each one, said yes to the recipes we liked and put the rest in a discard pile. The next step was to sort the keepers into piles that not only made sense but pleased us and said something meaningful about the food. In the end, we found we had identified what you might think of as the prevailing winds of The Vancouver Sun Test Kitchen.

We noticed that we had a lot of salmon recipes, a lot of berry desserts and an apparent preoccupation with new potatoes, and with the first jolt of recognition, the Home Grown chapter took shape: "Of course we cook this way, this is where we live." We also had a big pile of recipes for scones and muffins, some wonderfully stolid vegetable dishes and more ways to cook lamb than you could shake a stick at. "Rule Britannia," we said, and gazed into the eyes of the British past, still lively and chipper in the food we eat. Once those two categories were in place it was natural to look for food that would fit a Pacific Rim section. We grouped the salads, stir-fries and Asian-inspired recipes for the grill, and On the Rim materialized. The recipes that were left resolved themselves into the final two chapters: Italian, the most popular "ethnic" food in North America, and Chocolate, our obsession.

I wouldn't presume to tell you you'll love all of these recipes. But I suspect that you'll come to treasure a good handful of them. I make Barbecued Salmon with Sun-Dried Tomatoes all through the summer, and Herbed Green Beans. The quick pizza dough is an endless source of easy breads, as well as pizzas. I don't usually follow recipes for salads, but when I make a new potato salad, it often has the same flavors as New-Potato Salad with Basil and Sun-Dried Tomatoes. I have friends who swear by Salmon Misonese, who always have Roasted Red Peppers in Balsamic Vinegar on hand in the summer, and who like Orzo Salad with Snow Peas and Asparagus for picnics.

This way of cooking fits my life and the lives of people I know. That makes me feel confident in saying that the final answer to the question "What is Five-Star Food?" might be this: a modest but true picture of home cooking on Canada's West Coast.

Splendid Salmon

★

The Ultimate Home Brew: Soup

★

Potatoes, From Infancy Up

★

Berries, Cherries, Peaches, Apples, Pears

Why do people on the West Coast eat the way they do? A big part of the answer is sheer dumb luck. Here, in the midst of plenty, food from the sea and soil is magnificent, the equal of any in the world.

In the test kitchen we favor local produce, not just for patriotic reasons but because it's the best. Our strawberries put California imports to shame; our raspberries achieve a standard to which others only aspire. All berries like the soil here. Every summer trucks bring stone fruit from Okanagan orchards, picked ripe because it doesn't have to travel far. Later in the season come bright red McIntosh apples and a score of other varieties.

And then, of course, there's salmon, once the food that defined the people of the Northwest coast and still our emblem. What else would you serve to someone visiting from Toronto?

★ ★ ★ ★ ★

SPLENDID SALMON

On December 4, 1947, under the heading "Cottage Callers," The Vancouver Sun ran the results of an informal poll on the question: "What good dish do you think about first when B.C. cookery is mentioned?" Of 17 people who dropped in on Edith Adams on the day this question was asked, 12 answered "salmon." "Versatile," they said, and "delicious." "Looks good," said one caller. Another offered the oddly phrased "fresh food and good for one." Nowadays we might feel ourselves forced to disagree with M.F. Madill, of 4119 Dundas, whose patriotic answer – "baked stuffed salmon is the finest dish on earth" – still speaks to the home-loving heart. But if you ask any 17 people who live here what they think of first when B.C. food is mentioned, I suspect that at least 12 of them would answer: salmon. We love to cook it; we love to eat it. These are the best ways we've found.

Gravlax with Mustard and Dill Sauce

Makes 12 appetizer-size servings

Gravlax is cured salmon, as tender and melting as butter. We made this recipe as the appetizer for a West Coast Christmas menu, but there aren't many celebrations it wouldn't fit. Gravlax is easy to make. Just be sure to allow a couple of days for the uncooked salmon to cure. Start with fresh fish, and keep it refrigerated while it's curing.

3½ pounds (1.5 kg) fresh salmon (centre cut)
1 large bunch fresh dill, chopped coarse
¼ cup (50 mL) coarse (pickling) salt
¼ cup (50 mL) sugar
2 tablespoons (30 mL) white peppercorns, crushed
Mustard and dill sauce (see recipe, facing page)

Have the salmon filleted into two matching pieces.

Place one fillet, skin-side down, in deep glass, enamel or stainless-steel baking dish or casserole. Sprinkle dill over salmon.

Combine salt, sugar and crushed peppercorns. Sprinkle evenly over dill. Top with other half of the fish, skin-side up. Cover with aluminum foil and on it set a heavy platter slightly larger than the salmon. Pile the platter with three or four cans of food – these make convenient weights that are easy to distribute evenly. Place in refrigerator for 48 hours.

Turn fish every 12 hours, basting with liquid marinade that

GROW YOUR OWN DILL

Dill is an annual that likes full sun and rich, well-drained soil.

Sow seeds in the spring: for a supply of fresh leaves, sow a small amount of dill weekly. You'll get the best flavor from dill leaves picked just as the flowers are opening.

Fresh dill leaf can be frozen for later use. Wash, pat dry, store in freezer bags.

accumulates, separating the halves to baste the salmon inside. Replace platter and weights each time.

After 48 hours, remove fish from marinade, scrape away dill and seasoning and pat dry with paper towels. Place separated halves, skin-side down, on carving board and slice the salmon halves thinly on the diagonal, detaching each slice from the skin. Serve with mustard and dill sauce. (Recipe adjacent.) ★

MUSTARD AND DILL SAUCE

- **4 tablespoons (60 mL) old-fashioned grainy mustard**
- **1 teaspoon (5 mL) dry mustard**
- **3 tablespoons (45 mL) sugar**
- **2 tablespoons (30 mL) white vinegar**
- **⅓ cup (75 mL) vegetable oil**
- **3 tablespoons (45 mL) fresh dill, chopped fine**

In a small bowl, combine grainy mustard, dry mustard, sugar and vinegar. Slowly whisk in oil until mixture thickens. Stir in dill. Cover tightly and refrigerate. Just before serving, whisk sauce.

Smoked Salmon Torta

Makes about 3½ cups (875 mL)

The easiest party food of all is a side of smoked salmon, pre-sliced, with bagels, cream cheese, capers, sliced onions, a few branches of fresh thyme (for a garnish and to sprinkle over the salmon) and a bowl of lemon wedges. If your budget doesn't allow that much ease, here's an appetizer that combines the luxury and elegance of smoked salmon with a reasonable degree of economy. Serve it with crackers and slices of baguette.

- **2 (250-g) packages cream cheese, at room temperature**
- **½ cup (125 mL) butter, at room temperature**
- **Salt**
- **2 or 3 sprigs fresh dill**
- **¼ cup (50 mL) chopped fresh dill**
- **½ pound (250 g) sliced smoked salmon**
- **Assorted bread and crackers**

Beat together cream cheese and butter; add salt to taste. Line a 3½-cup (875-mL) straight-sided plain mould (loaf pan, terrine or charlotte mould) with a piece of plastic wrap large enough to extend over edge of mould. Arrange dill sprigs on bottom of mould.

Carefully spread one-third of the cheese mixture in mould to make an even layer. Sprinkle half the chopped dill over cheese layer; top with half the smoked salmon. Repeat layering, ending with cream cheese mixture. Press down lightly to compact layers. Cover and chill overnight.

To serve, dip mould in hot water for a few seconds. Pull edges of plastic wrap up to loosen torta; invert on to plate and carefully remove plastic wrap. Garnish as desired. ★

Cold Poached Salmon Steaks with Cream Cheese and Dill

Makes six servings

West Coast summers are rarely hot for long. But for a week or two, when scorching weather dulls appetites and drives cooks out of the kitchen, this elegant recipe will come in handy. Cook the fish in the morning and at dinner time you'll have nothing to do but make the sauce. Only self-indulgent cooks cool off by letting their arms linger inside the refrigerator.

- **3 cups (750 mL) chicken stock**
- **2½ to 3 pounds (1.25 to 1.5 kg) salmon steaks**
- **1 (250-g) container spreadable cream cheese**
- **2 tablespoons (30 mL) mayonnaise**
- **2 tablespoons (30 mL) milk**
- **1 teaspoon (5 mL) lemon juice**
- **½ teaspoon (2 mL) salt**
- **2 teaspoons (10 mL) chopped fresh dill OR ½ teaspoon (2 mL) dried dill weed**
- **2 to 3 drops Tabasco sauce**
- **1¼ cups (300 mL) chopped long English cucumber**
- **Lettuce**
- **Paprika**
- **Lemon wedges**

In large saucepan, heat chicken stock; add salmon steaks and poach gently until flesh is firm and opaque. Remove from poaching liquid and chill.

Beat together cream cheese, mayonnaise, milk, lemon juice, salt, dill and Tabasco sauce. Stir in cucumber and set aside.

Remove skin and bones from the salmon. Arrange the steaks on a lettuce-lined platter. Spoon cream cheese sauce over the fish and sprinkle with paprika. Garnish with lemon wedges and serve. ★

SPRING SALMON

Also called Chinook and King salmon, it is considered the top fish for the dinner table. The largest of the five species of Pacific salmon caught in B.C., its flesh is rich and oily, and separates into large flakes when cooked. Spring salmon can be deep red, pink or white, so don't let the standard color prejudice – red is best – stand in your way.

COHO SALMON

Firm textured, fatty, with a pink to red-orange flesh, Coho forms large flakes when cooked. Some rate Coho second only to Spring.

SOCKEYE SALMON

Red-fleshed, with a firm texture, Sockeye is moderately fatty and separates into fine flakes when cooked. At an average weight of five to seven pounds, it's a manageable size to bake or grill whole.

CHUM SALMON

Also called Dog salmon because they develop large teeth in spawning season, Chums have flesh that's white to pink in color, less fatty and less expensive than Spring, Coho or Sockeye.

PINK SALMON

The B.C. Salmon Marketing Council will tell you that Pink salmon, at a peak of freshness, is the equal on the dinner table of any other salmon. On the other hand, Pinks deteriorate rapidly. If you're not buying your salmon straight off the boat, its texture may be disappointing. At their best, Pinks have delicate pink flesh, are less oily than Sockeye or Chinook, and have a more subtle salmon flavor. They're also less expensive.

Salmon Fillets with Wine and Hazelnut-Cream Sauce

Makes four servings

Cliff Charron, chef and co-owner of Charron's, a restaurant in Campbell River, created this recipe combining two spectacular home-grown flavors: salmon and hazelnuts. Rich and proud of it, this is still a simple recipe you can make with ease for a modest company dinner. Serve it with buttered new potatoes, baby carrots and snow peas.

2 tablespoons (30 mL) butter or margarine
2 tablespoons (30 mL) olive oil
4 (6-ounce or 170-g) salmon fillets, skinned
½ cup (125 mL) flour
Salt and freshly ground pepper to taste
1 large garlic clove, chopped fine
1 small onion, chopped fine
3 tablespoons (45 mL) chopped roasted hazelnuts
¼ cup (50 mL) dry white wine
1 cup (250 mL) whipping cream
¼ teaspoon (1 mL) dried dill weed

Heat butter and olive oil in frypan. Dredge salmon fillets in flour. Fry in butter mixture until fish flakes easily when tested with a fork. Season with salt and pepper. Remove fillets from pan and keep warm.

In same frypan, fry garlic and onion until transparent. Add hazelnuts. Add wine and stir to loosen any brown bits off bottom of frypan. Stir in cream and dill. Cook until liquid is reduced by half. Season with salt and pepper. Place salmon in sauce and heat through. ★

Barbecued Salmon with Sun-Dried Tomatoes

Makes six to nine servings

Every time I cook salmon this way, I thank Vancouver fire-fighter David Veljacic, the competitive cook who took first place in a barbecued salmon contest with this recipe. It's fast, it's easy and people love it. You can, by the way, cheat on the length of time you leave the seasoning mixture in the refrigerator. Overnight is best, but if all you have is two hours, it's still worth making.

- **5 large garlic cloves, chopped fine**
- **3 tablespoons (45 mL) finely chopped fresh parsley**
- **3 sun-dried tomatoes (packed in oil), drained and chopped fine**
- **1 teaspoon (5 mL) salt**
- **¼ cup (50 mL) olive oil**
- **1 (2 to 3-pound or 1 to 1.5-kg) salmon fillet**

Combine garlic, parsley, sun-dried tomatoes, salt and olive oil in jar. Let stand overnight in refrigerator.

Place salmon, skin-side down, on large piece of greased foil; place over low heat on gas barbecue. Close top of barbecue and cook for 10 minutes.

With very sharp knife, cut two lengthwise slits in fillet, dividing the surface of the fish in thirds. Cut to the skin, but not through it.

Spread garlic mixture over fillet and into slits. Close top and raise temperature to medium. Cook for an additional 15 minutes or until fish flakes easily when tested with a fork. ★

WILD FISH WINS

Which is better, wild or farmed fish? We took the question into the test kitchen where two salmon, equal sizes, equally fresh, baked in foil with minimal seasoning, met 12 tasters.

Nine of the 12 were able to tell which fish was wild and which was farmed. The ocean-caught fish was described as having firmer flesh and a stronger taste.

One taster was poetic enough to mention "the wild, raw taste of freedom"; two others preferred the milder taste of the farmed salmon.

Savory Barbecued Salmon

Makes four servings

Fish and Co. restaurant, in the Hyatt Regency Vancouver, sells more salmon – poached, baked or grilled – than any other entree. Executive chef Othmar Steinhart gave us this easy barbecued salmon recipe; marinated overnight and then grilled, it gets rich flavor from surprisingly little effort. Serve it as a main course, or cook it, chill it, and make eight appetizer servings.

- **4 (6-ounce or 170-g) salmon fillets**
- **2 tablespoons (30 mL) horseradish**

2 tablespoons (30 mL) Dijon mustard
2 tablespoons (30 mL) oyster sauce
2 tablespoons (30 mL) chili sauce
2 tablespoons (30 mL) soy sauce
¼ cup (50 mL) dry white wine

Place salmon fillets in shallow baking dish. Combine remaining ingredients and pour over fish. Cover and refrigerate overnight.

Remove fillets from marinade and place on hot greased barbecue grill, flesh-side down; turn once and cook until fish flakes easily when tested with a fork.

Note: Fish may also be baked in a 450 F (230 C) oven for about 10 minutes per inch (2.5 cm) of thickness. ★

MORE ON MISO

Miso, a salty, aromatic paste made from fermented soybeans, is one of the most important ingredients in Japanese cooking.

If you're trying miso for the first time, a good rule of thumb is: the lighter the color, the milder the taste. There are three basic types of miso. Strong-flavored hatcho miso is dark, salty and pungent, made entirely from soybeans. Barley miso, usually golden in color and mild, is made from soybeans fermented with barley. And shiro or rice miso is a pale tan color, and the mildest of all.

Store any extra miso tightly covered in the refrigerator; it will keep several months. Freezing destroys the aroma and the texture.

Broiled Salmon Misonese

Makes four servings

Broiled salmon under a crust of miso paste and mayonnaise, topped with chopped chives is a Japanese-inspired approach to salmon created by chef Shun Ohnishi, then at the Cannery Restaurant.

Miso, a wickedly salty paste made from soybeans, is widely available in health food stores and progressive supermarkets.

6 tablespoons (90 mL) mayonnaise
1 tablespoon (15 mL) barley miso paste
2 tablespoons (30 mL) olive oil
2 teaspoons (10 mL) sesame oil
2 tablespoons (30 mL) chopped fresh chives, divided
¼ teaspoon (1 mL) salt
Pinch freshly ground pepper
4 (6-ounce or 170-g) salmon fillets

Mix together mayonnaise and miso paste; set aside.

Combine olive oil, sesame oil, one tablespoon (15 mL) chives, salt and pepper; drizzle on top of salmon fillets and spread to cover evenly.

Place fillets on broiler pan and broil until almost cooked. Spoon about one tablespoon (15 mL) mayonnaise mixture on top of each salmon fillet and broil for 1½ minutes. Garnish with remaining one tablespoon (15 mL) chives and serve immediately. ★

Salmon with Roasted Red Pepper Sauce

Makes six servings

The sweet, mellow flavor of roasted red pepper sauce is magnificent with grilled salmon and equally good with broiled or poached fish. To simplify the dinner hour, make the sauce a day ahead and gently warm it in the microwave while the fish is cooking.

6 salmon steaks, about 1-inch (2.5-cm) thick
3 tablespoons (45 mL) vegetable oil
2 tablespoons (30 mL) lemon juice

Red Pepper Sauce:

4 medium red bell peppers
1 tablespoon (15 mL) olive oil
1 tablespoon (15 mL) balsamic vinegar
Salt and freshly ground pepper to taste

For sauce: Broil red peppers on baking sheet, turning several times until skin is charred, about 20 to 25 minutes. Place in a brown paper bag. Close bag and let stand until peppers are cool enough to handle. Peel away the paper-thin skins, remove cores and rinse peppers under cold water to remove seeds. Drain on paper towels.

Place peppers, olive oil and vinegar in blender; process until smooth. Season with salt and pepper. Warm slightly before serving with salmon.

Brush salmon steaks lightly with mixture of vegetable oil and lemon juice. Place on greased barbecue grill or under broiler for about six to eight minutes per side or until fish flakes easily when tested with a fork. Serve with warm red pepper sauce. ★

Salmon with Tamarind Sauce

Makes four servings

Tamarind is an intensely sour pod used, among other things, to give Worcestershire sauce its characteristic flavor. Tamarind pulp comes in blocks, partially dried and wrapped in plastic – a dead ringer for packaged dried dates. Like packaged dates, dried tamarind blocks should be slightly soft to the touch and should look moist. Stephen Wong, who writes about the food of the Pacific Rim for our food pages, introduced us to tamarind in the flesh. Here it adds incomparable sweet-tartness to a sauce served with simple broiled salmon.

½ teaspoon (2 mL) salt
½ teaspoon (2 mL) ground turmeric
¼ teaspoon (1 mL) freshly ground pepper
4 (6-ounce or 170-g) salmon fillets
2 tablespoons (30 mL) vegetable oil, divided
2 teaspoons (10 mL) finely chopped garlic
2 tablespoons (30 mL) light soy sauce
1 tablespoon (15 mL) fish sauce
2 tablespoons (30 mL) brown sugar, about
¼ cup (50 mL) tamarind liquid (see explanation)
1 or 2 small fresh green chili peppers, sliced
3 tablespoons (45 mL) chopped green onions
Cilantro sprigs for garnish

Combine salt, turmeric and pepper. Rub each salmon fillet with some of the turmeric mixture. Lightly coat fillets with one tablespoon (15 mL) oil.

Place fillets, skin-side down, on lightly greased barbecue grill over medium heat; cook until fish flakes easily when tested with a fork. Place on a platter and keep warm.

In small stainless steel frypan, heat remaining one tablespoon (15 mL) oil over low heat. Add garlic and saute until lightly browned. Add soy sauce, fish sauce, sugar and tamarind liquid. Bring to a boil over medium heat and add more brown sugar if desired. Reduce heat and simmer about two minutes or until sauce is slightly thickened.

Add chili peppers and green onions to sauce and simmer for one minute to blend flavors. Pour evenly over fish and garnish with cilantro. ★

TREATING TAMARIND

To prepare tamarind for cooking, cut or break off a piece from the block and soak it in hot water in a glass or plastic bowl for about 15 minutes.

For a 1-inch (2.5-cm) cube of dried tamarind, use about ½ cup (125 mL) of water. (Wrap the remaining block tightly in plastic wrap and it will keep in your refrigerator for many months.)

After the tamarind has steeped, work the softened pulp with your fingers to separate the pulp from the fibres. Then strain the mixture through a fine sieve, pushing it with your fingers to extract all the liquid. Discard the fibrous mass and seeds.

You'll be left with a puree-like liquid, the form of tamarind that is generally called for in recipes. Keep excess tamarind liquid refrigerated. It will keep up to a week in a glass or plastic container.

The Ultimate Home Brew: Soup

It's a cliche, I know, to link soup and home. But I can't help it. It just so happens that the best soups we've made lately have all had a large measure of home in their ingredient list.

Corn, tomatoes, crab, shrimp, and, later in the year, carrots, cauliflower and parsnips: they all add a home-grown taste to the soups on our table. Some cooks avoid making soup because they can't see a place in their lives for a pot that simmers for hours on a back burner. Think again: one of these soups doesn't cook at all; the rest bubble gently for half an hour or less.

Fresh Corn and Crab Chowder

Makes six to eight servings

Chilliwack corn, sold by fresh-faced young boys in Granville Island Market on the same day it's picked, is one of summer's treasures. So is Dungeness crab meat. Together they make this one of season's best soups. We first sampled it in 1987, the year Eddy Cheung opened the Santa Fe restaurant and showed us how Southwestern we could be without ever leaving home.

- **3 large cobs of corn**
- **½ medium onion, chopped fine**
- **4 tablespoons (60 mL) unsalted butter, divided**
- **2 cups (500 mL) fish or chicken stock**
- **3 cups (750 mL) whipping cream**
- **1½ tablespoons (22 mL) cornstarch**
- **¼ pound (125 g) fresh crab meat**
- **Salt and white pepper to taste**

With a sharp knife, cut the corn kernels from the cobs; set aside.

In large heavy saucepan, saute onion in one tablespoon (15 mL) butter. Add corn kernels and stock; bring to a boil. Boil until liquid is reduced by one-quarter. Add cream and bring to boil.

In small saucepan, melt the remaining three tablespoons (45 mL) butter. Stir in cornstarch and cook for one minute; whisk into the soup until well blended. Add crab meat and salt and pepper to taste; heat through. ★

Fresh Tomato and Corn Soup with Basil and Parsley

Makes about six servings

Okanagan tomatoes, Chilliwack corn and the last of the garden's fresh basil make this the essential soup for early fall. Don't be put off by the idea of peeling tomatoes. Just drop them in boiling water and let stand for 10 to 15 seconds, then cool under cold water. The skins will slip off.

3 to 4 large ripe tomatoes
3 to 4 cobs of corn
3 tablespoons (45 mL) butter or margarine
½ cup (125 mL) chopped onion
½ cup (125 mL) chopped celery
¼ cup (50 mL) chopped green bell pepper
1 teaspoon (5 mL) finely chopped fresh basil
2 cups (500 mL) chicken stock
Salt and freshly ground pepper to taste
¼ teaspoon (1 mL) sugar, optional
2 tablespoons (30 mL) finely chopped fresh parsley
2 tablespoons (30 mL) thinly sliced green onions

Peel and chop tomatoes (should have four cups or 1 L). With a sharp knife, cut corn kernels from cobs (should have two cups or 500 mL).

In large heavy saucepan, melt butter over medium heat. Add onion, celery and green pepper; saute until tender but not browned, about five minutes. Add tomatoes and basil. Cover and cook for 20 minutes, stirring occasionally.

Press tomato mixture through sieve into large saucepan. Add chicken stock and salt and pepper; bring to a boil over medium-high heat. Add corn and bring to a boil. Reduce heat and simmer just until corn is tender, about three minutes. Add sugar if desired. Garnish with parsley and green onions. ★

COLD TOMATO

If your garden crop is massive, or you found a great end-of-season buy on vine-ripened tomatoes, you can freeze them with minimal preparation. Remove the core first, then pop tomatoes whole into plastic freezer bags.

When you want to use them, hold the frozen tomato under hot running water and the skins will crack and slip off easily. They won't have the texture of fresh tomatoes, but they'll be fine for most cooking purposes.

If you have a lot of tomatoes, or if freezer space is an issue, peel and quarter the tomatoes before cooking or cook them down into thick sauces before freezing.

★ ★ ★ ★ ★

Cold Buttermilk Shrimp Soup with Cumin and Dill

Makes about six servings

If you're looking for a low-fat summer soup that's festive enough to serve to dinner guests, this recipe is for you. For the freshest flavor, buy whole cumin seeds and grind them yourself just before you add them to the soup. (It's worth having an extra coffee grinder, just for spices.) For the richest cumin flavor, dry-roast the seeds in a frypan before you grind them.

1 pound (500 g) cooked shrimp
1 tablespoon (15 mL) chopped fresh dill
OR 1 teaspoon (5 mL) dried dill weed
½ teaspoon (2 mL) sugar
½ teaspoon (2 mL) Dijon mustard
¼ teaspoon (1 mL) ground cumin
¼ teaspoon (1 mL) salt
Pinch freshly ground pepper
½ long English cucumber
1 green onion, chopped (green part only)
1 tablespoon (15 mL) finely chopped green bell pepper
3 cups (750 mL) buttermilk
Snipped fresh dill for garnish, optional

In large bowl, combine shrimp, chopped dill, sugar, mustard, cumin, salt and pepper; let stand 30 minutes.

Cut cucumber into julienne strips, 1½ inches (4 cm) long. (You should have about one cup or 250 mL.) Add cucumber, onion and green pepper to shrimp mixture; toss. Stir in buttermilk. Cover and refrigerate until well chilled. Garnish with snipped dill if desired. ★

A PASSION FOR CUMIN

Cumin is an exotic spice with some much more familiar botanical cousins: parsley, dill, fennel and caraway. Roasting cumin intensifies its aroma and takes the sharp edges off its flavor. Pungent and intoxicating, it's a taste that can inspire passion.

My roasted cumin has a grinder all its own, standing by for a quick grind over potatoes, guacamole, corn on the cob, bean soups and sliced cucumbers. I'm fighting the urge to take it to the dinner table with the salt and pepper.

To roast cumin, use a heavy pan, on medium heat. Add the whole seeds, and roast for two to three minutes, shaking the pan frequently. The seeds should darken, but if they're black, they're burned. Throw them out and start over.

Roasted Carrot and Brie Soup

Makes about six servings

Roasted carrots are as sweet as candy. Combine them with brie and whipping cream and you have a luxurious winter soup. We found it on the menu at the Chateau Whistler Resort and asked executive chef Bernard Casavant for the recipe.

- **2 tablespoons (30 mL) butter or margarine**
- **3 cups (750 mL) coarsely chopped carrots**
- **½ cup (125 mL) coarsely chopped Spanish onions**
- **6 cups (1.5 L) chicken stock**
- **Salt and freshly ground pepper to taste**
- **3 ounces (75 g) brie cheese, rind removed**
- **¾ cup (175 mL) whipping cream**

Melt butter in 9-inch (23-cm) square baking pan in 450 F (230 C) oven. Add carrots and roast for 20 minutes or until lightly browned, stirring occasionally.

Transfer carrots and butter to large heavy saucepan. Add onions and cook until onions are translucent, about three to five minutes. Add chicken stock. Season with salt and pepper and simmer for 30 minutes or until carrots are soft.

Pour about one-third of the soup into blender. Cut cheese into small pieces and add to soup in blender; blend until smooth. Pour into a clean saucepan. Blend remaining soup and add to saucepan. Add cream and correct seasonings if necessary. ★

Cream of Cauliflower Soup with Cheddar Cheese and Dijon Mustard

Makes four to six servings

Fraser Valley farmers grow snowy white heads of cauliflower with a flavor more intense than anything you'll get trucked up from California. Here's a soup so easy you'll find yourself turning it into one of winter's staple dinners. Cook it from scratch in the microwave in less than half an hour.

1 small head cauliflower
2 tablespoons (30 mL) water
1 medium onion, chopped
¼ cup (50 mL) butter or margarine
4 cups (1 L) milk
⅓ cup (75 mL) all-purpose flour
1 teaspoon (5 mL) salt
1 cup (250 mL) grated cheddar cheese
2 teaspoons (10 mL) Dijon mustard

Cut cauliflower into bite-size flowerets. You should have about four cups (1 L).

Place cauliflower, water, onion and butter in three-quart (3-L) microwaveable casserole. Cover and microwave at HIGH (full power) for five to six minutes or until almost tender.

In bowl, whisk together milk, flour and salt, combining well. Stir into vegetables. Cover and microwave at HIGH for eight to nine minutes or until mixture boils and thickens, stirring two or three times.

Stir cheese and mustard into soup. Microwave at HIGH, uncovered, about one minute or until cheese is melted, stirring once. ★

Parsnip Soup with Fresh Thyme

Makes four to six servings

There are those who like parsnips, and those who don't. We're of the first persuasion, so we were delighted by Four Seasons chef Ian Cowley's smooth and voluptuous parsnip soup. Cowley starts his soup by sauteing the vegetables to concentrate their flavors and caramelize their natural sugars. The rice helps thicken the soup, cutting down on the amount of cream you need to make it deliciously creamy.

⅓ cup (75 mL) unsalted butter
4 medium parsnips, peeled and diced (½ inch or 1 cm)
¾ cup (175 mL) diced onions
1 sprig fresh thyme
¼ teaspoon (1 mL) sugar
¼ teaspoon (1 mL) salt
Freshly ground pepper to taste
5½ cups (1.375 L) chicken or vegetable stock
¼ cup (50 mL) white rice
⅔ cup (150 mL) whipping cream
Finely chopped fresh chives or parsley for garnish, optional

Heat butter in saucepan over medium-low heat. Add parsnips, onions, thyme, sugar, salt and pepper; saute, without browning, for about 10 to 15 minutes, stirring frequently.

Add stock and rice; bring to a boil. Reduce heat and simmer, uncovered, for 20 to 25 minutes. Remove thyme sprig and discard.

Puree soup in blender, in batches, until smooth; strain through sieve. Return to saucepan and stir in cream; heat through, stirring frequently (do not let boil). Garnish with chives if desired. ★

GROW YOUR OWN THYME

Common, or English thyme is the hardiest and most valuable in the kitchen, but there are more than 300 varieties, some with culinary uses, some without. Cooks with a sense of adventure can also grow caraway thyme, nutmeg thyme, lemon thyme and oregano thyme.

A perennial, thyme likes lots of sun and a light, well-drained, preferably alkaline soil.

It takes well to pots and is an easy plant to grow. Thyme gets woody after three or four years; you may want to replace it with new plants.

★ ★ ★ ★ ★

Potatoes, From Infancy Up

What charming infants they are, these baby potatoes, hand dug from the wet fields and offered as one of the first local crops every spring. These tender little spuds, with paper-thin skins that you needn't bother to peel, have the richest, freshest potato taste. At first, all we want to do is boil them, scatter fresh chives, mint, or parsley over the top, and add a pat of butter and a grinding of salt and pepper. Later, we start looking for something more elaborate, and variations of new-potato salad take up residence in our refrigerator. Eventually, even potatoes have to grow up. That's when we find ways to show off the rewards of maturity.

New-Potato and Snow Pea Salad

Makes eight servings

New potatoes, tossed in a mustard vinaigrette while they're still steaming, then tossed again with snow peas, sweet red peppers and green onions, make an exceptional early summer meal. Serve this salad warm or chilled, with a glass of wine, a few sun-dried black olives and a loaf of good bread.

Dressing:

- ¼ **cup (50 mL) white wine vinegar**
- 1 **garlic clove, crushed**
- 2 **tablespoons (30 mL) Dijon mustard**
- ½ **teaspoon (2 mL) salt**
- ¼ **teaspoon (1 mL) pepper**
- ½ **cup (125 mL) olive oil**

Salad:

- 3 **pounds (1.5 kg) new potatoes**
- ¼ **cup (50 mL) chopped green onions**
- 1 **cup (250 mL) snow peas, cut into small pieces**
- ½ **cup (125 mL) chopped red bell pepper**

For dressing: In large bowl, whisk together vinegar, garlic, mustard, salt and pepper. Gradually whisk in oil.

For salad: Scrub potatoes. Boil in salted water until just tender; drain. When cool enough to handle, cut into chunks. Add warm potatoes to dressing in bowl and mix until coated. Add green onions, snow peas and red pepper. Serve warm or refrigerate until ready to serve. ★

KEEP POTATOES YOUNG

Store potatoes in a dark, cool, well-ventilated cupboard; buy no more than you expect to use in two weeks.

New potatoes have a shorter shelf-life. Buy what you can use within four or five days. Store them in a paper bag in the refrigerator.

★ ★ ★ ★ ★

New-Potato Salad with Basil and Sun-Dried Tomatoes

Makes eight servings

Fragrant with fresh basil and studded with salty, intense bits of sun-dried tomatoes, this is potato salad gone continental. Serve it warm for the best flavor.

- **2½ pounds (1.25 kg) new potatoes**
- **¼ cup (50 mL) oil, drained from sun-dried tomatoes**
- **6 tablespoons (90 mL) vegetable oil**
- **6 tablespoons (90 mL) white wine vinegar**
- **2 teaspoons (10 mL) Dijon mustard**
- **2 garlic cloves, crushed**
- **1 teaspoon (5 mL) salt**
- **Pinch freshly ground pepper**
- **1 cup (250 mL) thinly sliced celery**
- **¼ cup (50 mL) slivered fresh basil**
- **⅔ cup (150 mL) thinly sliced green onions**
- **¼ cup (50 mL) slivered, drained sun-dried tomatoes (packed in oil)**

Scrub potatoes. Boil in salted water until just tender; drain and let cool.

Meanwhile prepare dressing. Place the ¼ cup (50 mL) oil from sun-dried tomatoes, vegetable oil, vinegar, mustard, garlic, salt and pepper in small bowl. Whisk until blended.

Peel and cut potatoes into ½-inch (1-cm) cubes. Place in large bowl and add half the dressing; mix lightly. Add celery, basil, green onions, sun-dried tomatoes and remaining dressing; mix lightly. Cover and chill if not serving shortly. Bring to room temperature before serving. ★

GROW YOUR OWN BASIL

Basil is the most tender of the kitchen herbs, with no tolerance at all for cold nights. On the West Coast, that means you shouldn't even consider planting it before the May 24th weekend; and if it's a cold spring, hold off a little longer.

Basil's an annual. It likes full sun and rich, moist soil. Pinch the stem tips frequently and it will bush out.

Bush basil is a particularly good variety to grow indoors on a sunny window sill.

Denny Boyd's Garlic New Potatoes

Makes four servings

Vancouver Sun columnist Denny Boyd is a man about the kitchen with a passion for new potatoes. His favorite recipe, with its half-cup of butter – or more if you like – isn't health food. But as a once a year indulgence, it won't hurt you. Besides, 12 cloves of garlic surely have some curative powers. And no, that isn't too much garlic. Because the cloves are left whole they don't overpower the potatoes.

1⅓ pounds (650 g) small new potatoes
8 to 12 garlic cloves, unpeeled
½ to ¾ cup (125 to 175 mL) butter

Wash potatoes in a sieve under cold running water. Place potatoes, garlic and butter in small saucepan with a tight-fitting lid.

Cover and place over medium to low heat, just hot enough to get the butter bubbling and simmering. Cook for 20 to 25 minutes or until potatoes are tender, occasionally shaking the pan. Listen for gentle bubbling in the pan. If it is loud, lower the heat. ★

GARLIC GUIDANCE

Buy garlic bulbs that are plump and firm. Squeeze one before you buy; it shouldn't give under your fingers.

Don't refrigerate garlic. Store it in a cool, dry place, in a container with good air circulation – either a ceramic garlic pot or a wicker or wire basket.

If you have one or two garlic cloves to peel, press the cloves against a cutting board with the flat side of a heavy knife: the skin will slip off.

To peel a whole head, cut the top quarter inch off and pop the whole head into the microwave for 15 to 20 seconds. The individual cloves will slip out of their skins with amazing ease.

★ ★ ★ ★ ★

Mashed Potato with Parsnip, Parsley and Chives

Makes eight servings

If you must feed eight people at a time, it helps to have in your repertoire a knockout vegetable dish that can be made ahead and reheated just before serving. This gussied-up version of mashed potatoes gets its sweetness from parsnips.

4 pounds (2 kg) potatoes, peeled and quartered
1½ pounds (750 g) parsnips, peeled and cut into large pieces
½ cup (125 mL) butter or margarine
½ cup (125 mL) finely chopped green onions
½ cup (125 mL) milk (about), heated
Salt and freshly ground pepper to taste
2 tablespoons (30 mL) chopped fresh parsley
2 tablespoons (30 mL) chopped fresh chives (optional)

Bring large pot of lightly salted water to a boil over high heat. Add potatoes and boil for 10 minutes. Add parsnips and boil 10 minutes more or until parsnips and potatoes are tender.

Meanwhile, melt butter in small saucepan over low heat. Add green onions and cook over medium-low heat until softened, about two minutes.

Drain potatoes and parsnips; return them to the pot and heat for about one minute, tossing to let all excess moisture evaporate.

Mash potatoes and parsnips. Slowly stir in about ½ cup (125 mL) milk until smooth. Stir in green onions with butter. Add salt and pepper. Stir in parsley and chives.

Spoon into 2½-quart (2.5-L) serving dish and sprinkle with additional chopped parsley if desired.

Note: Can be made ahead and placed in 2½-quart (2.5-L) microwaveable casserole; cover and refrigerate. To reheat, microwave, covered, at HIGH (full power), for about 10 minutes or until heated through, stirring every four minutes. ★

GROW YOUR OWN PARSLEY

Parsley is a biennial that flowers in its second year. The leaves get bitter when the flower stalks form.

Parsley likes full sun, but will grow in light shade, and unlike most herbs prefers a rich, wet soil.

To freeze parsley: separate the leaves from the stems, chop fine. Store in freezer bags for up to one year.

Pommes Sautees a Cru

Makes two servings

Part of a spring dinner planned and executed in our kitchen by Thierry Damilano of Chez Thierry, the Lower Mainland's most cheerfully romantic French restaurant, these wonderful, crisp potatoes are just this side of potato chips. Flecked with parsley, shallot and raw garlic, they're amazingly good.

1 medium russet potato
Olive oil
1 shallot, chopped fine
1 garlic clove, chopped fine
1 tablespoon (15 mL) chopped fresh parsley
Salt and freshly ground pepper to taste

Peel potato, cut in half lengthwise and slice very thin crosswise. Place in bowl of cold water to prevent browning. Drain well on a clean tea towel before cooking.

In very large frypan, add olive oil to a depth of ⅛ inch (2.5 mm). Place pan over medium-high heat until oil is very hot. Add drained potatoes, spreading them out well in the pan. Cook until golden, shaking the frypan occasionally. Turn potatoes and cook on the other side. Be careful not to burn.

Remove with slotted spoon. Place in warm bowl. Add shallot, garlic, parsley, salt and pepper. Toss to coat well. ★

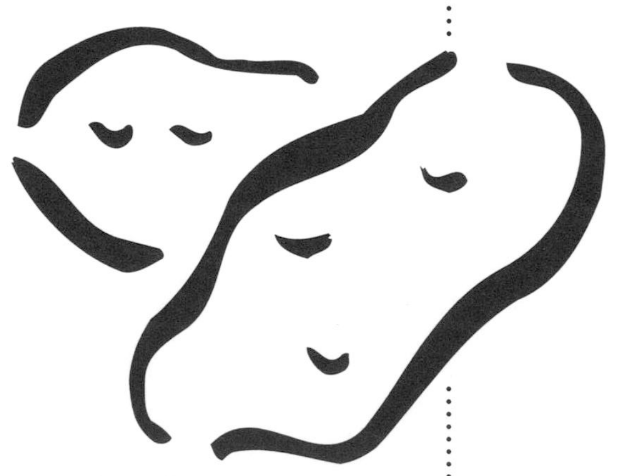

POTATO HORRORS

I hated going downstairs to get potatoes for supper when I was small. The dark cupboard, the dank smell, the one horrid old spud sprouting in the back with evil glowing in its pale shoots: beyond gross.

Turns out, my instincts were right. Potato sprouts are out to get you, and potatoes with a pale wash of green under the skin are too. Both have abnormally high levels of two chemicals normally found in potatoes: solanine and chaconine. Eat enough and you'll get sick.

If you find yourself staring down a pound or two of potatoes that are sprouting or green, either toss them in the compost or cut away the poison. Dig the sprouts out; don't just break them off. Peel green potatoes deeply.

Artichoke Potato au Gratin

Makes four to six servings

Artichokes can be intimidating. Don't let them get to you. Follow the directions – they'll make more sense when you have an artichoke in front of you – and you'll soon be an expert. With garlic, thyme and potatoes, artichokes make a substantial and richly flavored vegetable dish. Serve it with lamb or broiled chicken, or as the centrepiece of a vegetarian meal.

3 medium artichokes
4 to 6 cups (1 to 1.5 L) water
2 tablespoons (30 mL) lemon juice
1 tablespoon (15 mL) chopped garlic
2 teaspoons (10 mL) dried thyme, crushed
¾ teaspoon (4 mL) salt
⅛ teaspoon (0.5 mL) pepper
3 medium potatoes (unpeeled), sliced thin
3 tablespoons (45 mL) olive oil, divided
½ cup (125 mL) hot chicken or vegetable stock
½ cup (125 mL) soft bread crumbs

Bend back outer petals of artichokes until they snap off easily near base. Edible portion of petals should remain on artichokes. Continue to snap off and discard petals until central core of pale green petals is reached. Trim outer dark green layer from artichoke. Cut off stems and top one-third of artichokes, discard.

Quarter artichokes lengthwise. Cut out fuzzy centres. Slice each quarter lengthwise into three or four wedges. Combine water and lemon juice; add artichoke wedges.

Combine garlic, thyme, salt and pepper. Place layer of potato slices on bottom of greased 2½-quart (2.5-L) casserole. Remove artichokes from lemon-water. Cover potatoes with layer of artichoke wedges. Sprinkle with one heaping teaspoon (5 mL) garlic mixture and drizzle with one tablespoon (15 mL) oil. Repeat layers, ending with potato layer.

Pour stock evenly over surface, sprinkle with bread crumbs and drizzle with remaining one tablespoon (15 mL) oil. Cover and bake at 425 F (220 C) for 30 minutes. Uncover and bake another 10 to 20 minutes or until potatoes and artichokes are tender. ★

★ ★ ★ ★ ★

Berries, Cherries, Peaches, Apples, Pears:

Ways to Paint the Lily and Throw Perfume on the Violet

No berry tastes as good as the one you eat in the berry patch, warm from the sun. One of the great joys of living in the Lower Mainland is that the largest raspberry acreage in North America is within easy striking distance, and U-pick farms let you pick to your heart's content. Even if you can't get to the field, raspberries get to good produce markets on the same day they're picked – a big advantage to the most fragile of all berries.

But here the whole summer is a succession of berries, starting with strawberries, ending with wild blackberries in the fall. Along with the berries come Okanagan fruit: the sweetest peaches, the most flavorful nectarines, the juiciest apples. So all summer, we cook fruit desserts. Some of them are nutritionally impeccable paragons of low-fat eating. Others are shameless examples of gilding the lily and casting perfume on the violet. They're all easy and all spectacular.

Summertime Fruit Flan

Makes 12 servings

Once you've made this recipe a few times it becomes a habit. All summer long, you'll be turning fruits, berries and all combinations thereof into flans. This one is especially easy because it doesn't involve rolling out pastry. Make it a day ahead, then add the fruit and apricot glaze a few hours before serving.

Pastry:

- **½ cup (125 mL) butter or margarine, at room temperature**
- **1¾ cups (425 mL) sifted cake and pastry flour**
- **¼ cup (50 mL) icing sugar**

Filling:

- **1 (250-g) package cream cheese, at room temperature**
- **1 (125-g) package cream cheese, at room temperature**
- **¾ cup (175 mL) sifted icing sugar**
- **1½ teaspoons (7 mL) vanilla**
- **¾ cup (175 mL) whipping cream**
- **3 cups (750 mL) fresh fruit (see note)**

Glaze:

- **1 cup (250 mL) apricot jam**
- **4 teaspoons (20 mL) lemon juice**

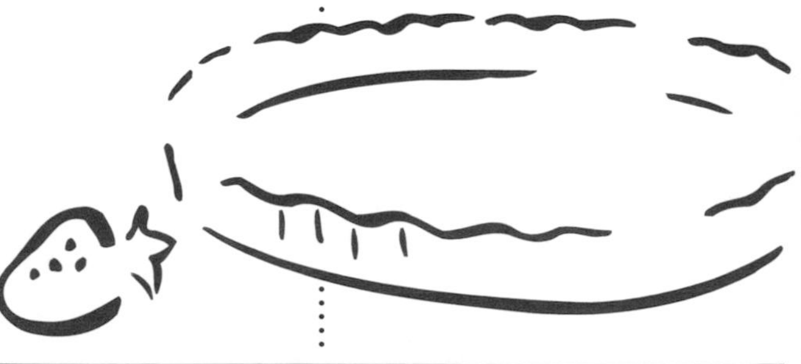

EASY FREEZING FOR PIES

If you like berry pies in the dead of winter, plan ahead. Here's an easy way to make your own frozen pie fillings at the peak of berry season.

Fill a freezer bag with a mixture of berries and slightly more thickener than you normally use. Press the freezer bag filled with berries into the pie plate, and put the pie plate in the freezer. When the berries are solid, remove the pie plate, wrap and label the pie filling.

For pastry: In bowl, cream butter. Gradually beat in flour and icing sugar. Press evenly into 11-inch (28-cm) flan pan; prick well with a fork. Bake at 425 F (220 C) for seven to 10 minutes, or until lightly browned.

For filling: In large bowl, beat both packages of cream cheese, icing sugar and vanilla together until smooth. In separate bowl, whip cream until stiff; fold into cheese mixture. Spread evenly in prepared shell. Chill until set, about one hour. Arrange fruit on top of cream cheese mixture.

For glaze: In saucepan, combine jam and lemon juice. Heat until jam melts, then press through sieve. Brush or spoon glaze over fruit. Chill.

Note: For fruit, use halved strawberries, raspberries, blueberries, sliced peeled peaches or sliced nectarines. ★

Many-Berry Sauce for Cake

Makes 10 servings

Cake and sauce is an easy and elegant dessert, and no one said you had to bake the cake. If you want to keep the fat content low, buy or bake an angel food. If you're inclined towards a richer indulgence, then try this sauce on pound cake.

- **3 cups (750 mL) fresh strawberries, sliced thick**
- **1 cup (250 mL) frozen unsweetened blueberries, partially thawed**
- **1 (300-g) package frozen unsweetened raspberries, thawed**
- **1 cup (250 mL) seedless red raspberry jam**
- **2 tablespoons (30 mL) orange-flavored liqueur**
- **2 teaspoons (10 mL) lemon juice**
- **Fresh mint leaves for garnish**

Place strawberries and blueberries in bowl.

Drain raspberries, reserving juice. In blender or food processor, blend raspberries and jam until smooth. Strain puree through sieve into small bowl. Stir in liqueur and lemon juice. If sauce is too thick, thin with a little reserved raspberry juice. Pour sauce over berries in bowl and stir.

Serve sauce over angel food cake or pound cake. Garnish with mint. ★

Mascarpone with Raspberry Puree

Makes four servings

It's amazing that something so rich can be so simple to make. Start with the best berries you can find, puree them, and add them to mascarpone – the Italian cream cheese that's sometimes described as similar to Devonshire clotted cream or French petit suisse. If the food budget won't permit imported mascarpone, look for a less expensive domestic mascarpone.

1 cup (250 mL) fresh raspberries
½ pound (250 g) mascarpone cheese
2 tablespoons (30 mL) sugar
½ teaspoon (2 mL) vanilla
Raspberries for garnish

Puree raspberries in blender or food processor. Press through fine sieve to remove seeds.

In bowl, beat together mascarpone, sugar, vanilla and raspberry puree with an electric mixer until smooth and fluffy. Spoon into individual dessert dishes and garnish with whole raspberries. Refrigerate at least one hour before serving.

Note: A ½ pound (250 g) of mascarpone cheese measures one cup (250 mL). ★

AVOID JAMMING-OUT

After a day spent picking berries, you may not feel like making several batches of jam. The good news is, you don't have to.

Use a potato masher to crush the berries you've decided to devote to jam, check your recipe and freeze the berries in bags or containers in the amount needed for each batch. Then, on some quiet autumn weekend, defrost the berries and make your jam.

Raspberries with Lavender Cream

Makes four servings

Come July, the heat is on to find as many ways to eat fresh raspberries as there are days in the regrettably short local season. Anthony Hodda, former chef at The Raintree Restaurant, provided us with this simple and startling recipe. His bold combination of raspberries with lavender-flavored creme anglaise is one of our favorites. If you don't have any lavender flowering in your own garden, ask a neighbor or friend. It's a popular plant with West Coast gardeners.

½ cup (125 mL) sugar
4 large egg yolks
12 stems fresh lavender
1¾ cups (425 mL) whipping cream, divided
1 cup (250 mL) light cream
Lemon wedge
Sugar
4 cups (1 L) fresh raspberries
Lavender for garnish

In bowl, whisk together ½ cup (125 mL) sugar and egg yolks; set aside.

Strip flowers from stems. Mix one cup (250 mL) whipping cream, light cream and flowers in heavy stainless steel saucepan. Slowly bring to a boil.

Stir cream mixture into egg yolk mixture, combining well. Return to saucepan and cook over low heat, stirring constantly, until mixture is thick enough to coat back of metal spoon, about 15 minutes. Strain into bowl and cool on rack. Cover and chill.

Whip remaining ¾ cup (175 mL) whipping cream.

Rub the rims of four martini glasses with a lemon wedge to moisten. Dip rims in sugar.

For each dessert, spoon about one tablespoon (15 mL) whipped cream into bottom of glass. Top with one cup (250 mL) raspberries. Pour ¼ cup (50 mL) lavender cream over berries. Garnish each dessert with some of the remaining whipped cream and lavender. (Extra lavender cream will keep several days in the refrigerator.) ★

GROW YOUR OWN LAVENDER

Lavender likes sunny, open spots with light, fast-draining soil.

Trim lavender after it flowers to keep the plants compact and neat.

English lavender blooms in July and August; French lavender has a longer flowering season, but is not as hardy.

Raspberry Almond Cream

Makes six servings

Raspberries and almonds are a particularly happy couple. And one of the easiest ways to bring them together is this creamy sauce flavored with amaretto liqueur. You can make the sauce ahead and keep it in the refrigerator for up to six hours.

1 (125-g) package cream cheese
½ cup (125 mL) icing sugar
2 tablespoons (30 mL) amaretto liqueur
¾ cup (175 mL) whipping cream
3 cups (750 mL) fresh raspberries

In large bowl, beat together cream cheese, sugar and liqueur until smooth. Continue beating and pour in cream in a steady stream. (Mixture should be the consistency of whipped cream at all times; if it looks soft, stop adding cream and continue to beat until mixture thickens.)

Line bottom of each of six dessert bowls with ⅓ cup (75 mL) of raspberries. Mound almond cream equally over each, then top with remaining berries. ★

CHEESY TRICK

If you're ready to cook, but the cream cheese isn't, let the microwave bring it to room temperature. Take off the wrapper, set the cream cheese on a plate, cover tightly.

If you're softening a 250-g package of cream cheese, microwave at HIGH for about 30 seconds.

Cherry-Blueberry Tart with Orange Pastry

Makes 10 to 12 servings

What do you do when the produce stalls overflow with ripe local cherries and berries? Start combining them. This elegant tart with its orange-flavored pastry, pairs cherries and blueberries. It's a perfect company dinner dessert, especially because you make it the day before you plan to serve it.

Orange pastry:

1½ cups (375 mL) all-purpose flour
2 tablespoons (30 mL) sugar
¼ teaspoon (1 mL) salt
½ cup (125 mL) cold butter or margarine
3 tablespoons (45 mL) thawed frozen orange juice concentrate

Filling:

- ½ **cup (125 mL) sugar**
- 3 **tablespoons (45 mL) cornstarch**
- ¼ **teaspoon (1 mL) salt**
- 2 **cups (500 mL) milk**
- 2 **large eggs**
- ¼ **teaspoon (1 mL) almond extract**

Topping:

- 3 **tablespoons (45 mL) sugar**
- 1 **tablespoon (15 mL) cornstarch**
- ½ **cup (125 mL) orange juice**
- 3 **cups (750 mL) fresh sweet cherries, pitted**
- 1½ **cups (375 mL) fresh blueberries, divided**

For pastry: In bowl, combine flour, sugar and salt. Cut in butter with a pastry blender until mixture resembles coarse crumbs. Stir in orange juice concentrate; using hands, gather into a ball.

Roll out pastry and fit into 11-inch (28-cm) flan pan; prick in several places with a fork. Put in freezer until firm, about 20 to 30 minutes. Bake at 425 F (220 C) for about 15 minutes or until golden. Cool.

For filling: In saucepan, combine sugar, cornstarch and salt. Stir in milk and cook over medium-high heat for about five minutes or until thickened, stirring constantly. In bowl, beat eggs. Add a small amount of hot milk mixture to eggs, stirring constantly. Add eggs to hot milk mixture, stirring constantly. Cook over medium heat until thickened, stirring constantly. Stir in almond extract. Cool.

For topping: In saucepan, combine sugar and cornstarch; stir in orange juice. Add cherries and ½ cup (125 mL) blueberries. Cook and stir over medium heat until thickened; stir in remaining blueberries. Cool.

Spread filling over bottom of pastry shell. Spoon cherry mixture over top and place in refrigerator overnight. ★

GUILTY PASTRY SECRET

The most heartfelt tip I can give you on the subject of pie crusts is this: keep a box of pie-crust mix in the cupboard. When there's a need for pastry, all you have to do is add water and roll it out. It's fast and it's consistently good.

But what happens when you need or want to make pastry from scratch? Take a deep breath, remind yourself that it's not brain surgery, then repeat, like a mantra: cold and light, cold and light.

- *Cold hands, cold water, cold butter or lard: they all contribute to flaky pastry.*
- *Over-handled pastry gets tough. Practise lightness: just enough handling to make the dough form a compact ball; a gentle touch with the rolling pin, working from the centre to the edge.*

Lemon Blueberry Pizza

Makes eight to 10 servings

Yes, we're using the term pizza loosely here. But what else would you call this blueberry dessert with its graham wafer crust and creamy, fruity filling?

Lemon Crumb Crust:

- ½ **cup (125 mL) melted butter or margarine**
- 1 **tablespoon (15 mL) lemon juice**
- 2½ **cups (625 mL) graham wafer crumbs**

Topping:

- ½ **cup (125 mL) granulated sugar**
- 3 **tablespoons (45 mL) cornstarch**
- 1¼ **cups (300 mL) water**
- 1½ **cups (375 mL) blueberries**
- 1 **tablespoon (15 mL) lemon juice**

Filling:

- 1 **(250-g) package cream cheese**
- 3 **tablespoons (45 mL) icing sugar**
- 2 **teaspoons (10 mL) grated lemon rind**
- 1 **cup (250 mL) whipping cream**
- 3 **cups (750 mL) blueberries**

For crust: In bowl, combine butter and lemon juice. Add crumbs and mix well. Pat evenly over bottom and sides of 12-inch (30.5-cm) pizza pan. Bake at 350 F (180 C) for five minutes. Let cool.

For topping: In saucepan, combine granulated sugar and cornstarch. Stir in water and berries. Cook over medium heat, stirring, until mixture boils and becomes thick and clear. Remove from heat and stir in lemon juice. Set aside to cool slightly.

For filling: In small bowl, beat cream cheese, icing sugar and lemon rind until fluffy. With mixer at high speed, slowly pour in cream and beat until well combined. Spread cream mixture evenly over crust. Top with berries.

Spoon slightly cooled topping over berries. Cover and chill until set, about one hour. ★

BE PREPARED FOR BERRIES

Before you go berry picking, lay in a stock of freezer bags. Round up a few litre-sized freezer containers and get out every cookie sheet you own.

Freeze strawberries, raspberries, blackberries, boysenberries and loganberries in single layers on cookie trays. When the berries are solid, bag them in freezer bags, suck out any air with a straw, and seal them.

Blueberries can just be bagged and frozen; no initial freezing is needed.

Amaretto Cheesecake with Fresh Peaches

Makes eight servings

It's remarkable what you can do with a microwave oven – keep the kitchen cool on a hot day and still serve a baked cheesecake for dessert, for example. Here, the almond flavoring goes particularly well with sliced fresh peaches, but try other toppings if you like. Use the food processor, if you have one, for chopping the nuts, but be careful not to overdo it: they should be chopped, not ground.

¼ cup (50 mL) butter or margarine
2 cups (500 mL) finely chopped almonds
2 tablespoons (30 mL) sugar
1 (250-g) package cream cheese
1 (125-g) package cream cheese
½ cup (125 mL) sugar
3 large eggs
1 cup (250 mL) dairy sour cream
2 tablespoons (30 mL) amaretto liqueur
½ teaspoon (2 mL) vanilla extract
½ teaspoon (2 mL) almond extract
Sliced fresh peaches

Place butter in 9½-inch (24-cm) microwaveable deep-dish pie plate or round baking dish. Microwave at HIGH (full power) for one to 1½ minutes or until butter is melted.

Stir in almonds and the two tablespoons (30 mL) sugar mixing until almonds are evenly coated with butter. Press nuts on to bottom and sides of pie plate. Microwave at HIGH for 1½ to two minutes or until firm. Set aside.

Place both packages of cream cheese in large microwaveable bowl and microwave at HIGH for 20 to 30 seconds or until softened. Add the ½ cup (125 mL) sugar and beat until light. Beat in eggs, one at a time. Add sour cream, liqueur and vanilla and almond extract; beat until smooth. Pour into baked crust.

Microwave at MEDIUM (half power) for 14 to 16 minutes or until cheesecake is just set in centre, rotating dish part way through cooking if necessary. Cool to room temperature, then cover and refrigerate until serving time.

Serve with sliced peaches (sweetened with a little sugar if desired). ★

French Apple Tarte

Makes eight to 10 servings

Fall is apple season, and when the new-crop apples arrive in the market the temptation to make an apple pie is irresistible. Readers request this superb French Apple Tarte again and again. A bonus: it has a press-in pastry and a crumbly topping, so it holds no fear for the pastry-phobic. If you're planning a company dinner, you can bake it the night before, then warm it slightly before serving.

Pastry:

- **1⅓ cups (325 mL) all-purpose flour**
- **3 tablespoons (45 mL) icing sugar**
- **⅔ cup (165 mL) butter or margarine, at room temperature**

Filling:

- **¾ cup (175 mL) granulated sugar**
- **2 tablespoons (30 mL) flour**
- **½ teaspoon (2 mL) ground cinnamon**
- **¼ teaspoon (1 mL) salt**
- **2 tablespoons (30 mL) butter or margarine, at room temperature**
- **7 cups (1.75 L) thinly sliced peeled apples**

Topping:

- **1¼ cups (300 mL) all-purpose flour**
- **½ cup (125 mL) packed brown sugar**
- **⅓ cup (75 mL) butter or margarine, at room temperature**

For pastry: In small bowl, combine flour and icing sugar. With pastry blender, cut in butter until crumbly. Press dough over bottom and 2 inches (5 cm) up the side of 9-inch (23-cm) springform pan; chill in refrigerator while preparing filling.

For filling: In large bowl, combine granulated sugar, flour, cinnamon and salt. With pastry blender, cut in butter until crumbly. Add apples; toss to coat. Place apple mixture in prepared crust.

For topping: In small bowl, combine flour and brown sugar. With pastry blender, cut in butter. Squeeze handfuls of topping into firm chunks; break chunks apart into smaller pieces. Sprinkle over surface of apples.

Bake at 350 F (180 C) for 60 to 75 minutes or until apples are tender, covering loosely with foil during last 20 minutes of baking to prevent over browning. Cool completely. ★

AN APPLE FOR EVERY DAY

McIntosh apples are great for eating and make wonderful applesauce. But they lose their shape and turn to mush in pies and crisps.

Red Delicious is an eating apple only; it's mushy and insipid cooked. Golden Delicious is good in pies.

Jonagold, like McIntosh, makes wonderful applesauce and mushy pies.

Cox's Orange Pippin, an old variety newly available in markets, has great taste in baking and holds its shape.

Spartan is a good apple for eating and for cooking.

Granny Smith, a widely available import, reaches its zenith in pies.

Apple Phyllo Squares

Makes eight to 10 servings

Use good, tart cooking apples to make this easy-going cousin of an apple strudel. Phyllo dough can be found in most grocery stores, usually in the freezer section. If you haven't used phyllo before, relax. The secret is to make sure that the dough is thoroughly defrosted, but not dried out. Once it's supple, keep it covered with a damp dishtowel.

8 cups (2 L) thinly sliced peeled apples
1 teaspoon (5 mL) grated lemon rind
2 tablespoons (30 mL) lemon juice
1 tablespoon (15 mL) brandy
½ cup (125 mL) dark brown sugar
2 tablespoons (30 mL) flour
½ teaspoon (2 mL) ground cinnamon
Pinch ground nutmeg
6 sheets frozen phyllo dough, thawed
¼ cup (50 mL) melted butter or margarine, about
¼ cup (50 mL) apricot jam

Place apples in large bowl. Add lemon rind, lemon juice and brandy and stir to coat apples well; set aside. In small bowl, stir together sugar, flour, cinnamon and nutmeg; set aside.

Brush bottom and sides of 13x9-inch (33x23-cm) baking pan with butter. Line pan with one sheet of phyllo, allowing edges of pastry to extend up the sides and beyond the edges of the pan; brush sides of phyllo with butter. Repeat with remaining sheets of phyllo, brushing last sheet completely with butter.

Add sugar mixture to apple mixture; stir to coat apples well. Spread evenly in prepared pan. Roll up phyllo to meet apples, forming an edge around pan. Brush edge with melted butter.

Bake at 350 F (180 C) for about 30 minutes or until apples are tender, brushing pastry edge with butter every 10 minutes.

In small saucepan, heat jam until it melts; strain. Brush over hot apple square. Cut in squares and serve warm or at room temperature. ★

Fresh Pear Custard Flan with Rosé Sauce

Makes six servings

When it's time to pull out all the stops with an elegant fruit dessert, try this one. Fresh pears, lightly caramelized in butter and sugar, form the bottom layer. They're covered with a creamy baked custard, and, as a final, rich touch, a rosé wine sauce flavored with lemon rind, cinnamon and currant jelly. The best pears for baking are firm and slightly underripe.

2 pounds (1 kg) firm fresh pears, peeled and cored
2 tablespoons (30 mL) butter or margarine
½ cup (120 mL) sugar, divided
3 large eggs
1⅓ cups (325 mL) light cream
1 tablespoon (15 mL) flour
1 teaspoon (5 mL) vanilla
⅛ teaspoon (0.5 mL) ground nutmeg

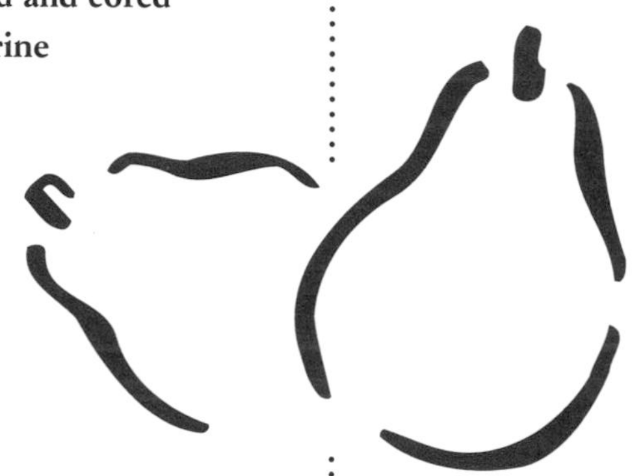

Sauce:

⅔ cup (150 mL) rosé wine
⅓ cup (75 mL) sugar
1 cinnamon stick
1 (1-inch or 2.5-cm) piece lemon rind
1 teaspoon (5 mL) cornstarch
⅓ cup (75 mL) red currant jelly

Cut pears into eighths. Melt butter in large frypan; add pears and three tablespoons (45 mL) sugar. Saute pears until most of the syrup has evaporated and pears are light gold in color. Transfer pears to 9-inch (23-cm) round cake pan.

In bowl, combine remaining five tablespoons (75 mL) sugar, eggs, cream, flour, vanilla and nutmeg; mix until well blended and pour over pears. Bake at 350 F (180 C) for 45 minutes or until a knife inserted in centre comes out clean. Cool to room temperature.

For sauce: In saucepan, combine wine, sugar, cinnamon stick and lemon rind. Bring to a boil and simmer for 15 minutes. Remove rind and cinnamon stick. In a cup, combine cornstarch and a few tablespoons of the wine mixture; stir until smooth. Add cornstarch mixture and currant jelly to hot wine mixture. Cook until syrup thickens. Remove from heat and set aside to cool.

Cut flan into wedges and serve with cooled sauce. ★

★ ★ ★ ★ ★

Pear Upside-Down Gingerbread

Makes six servings

Gingerbread is a homey affair, simple to make and endlessly satisfying. This dramatic version, which joins pears and ginger in a particularly inspired union, is best served warm with whipped cream.

3 small pears, peeled and halved
1¼ cups (300 mL) all-purpose flour
¾ teaspoon (4 mL) baking soda
1 teaspoon (5 mL) ground cinnamon
½ teaspoon (2 mL) ground ginger
¼ teaspoon (1 mL) ground cloves
½ teaspoon (2 mL) salt
½ cup (125 mL) buttermilk
¼ cup (50 mL) soft shortening
¼ cup (50 mL) sugar
1 large egg
½ cup (125 mL) table molasses
¼ cup (50 mL) chopped nuts
Whipped cream or ice cream for topping

Place pear halves, cut-side down and stem end toward centre, in well-greased 9-inch (23-cm) round cake pan; set aside.

In large bowl, combine flour, baking soda, cinnamon, ginger, cloves and salt. In blender or food processor, blend buttermilk, shortening, sugar, egg and molasses until smooth, about two minutes. Pour over dry ingredients and mix thoroughly.

Pour batter over pears and sprinkle with nuts. Bake at 350 F (180 C) for 40 to 45 minutes. Loosen cake from edges of pan and invert immediately on to serving plate. Serve warm, topped with whipped cream. ★

WHIPPING CREAM INTO SHAPE

First, be sure to start with cream that has at least 30 per cent butterfat.

Keep it cold. Put the beaters and the bowl in the freezer an hour or so before you plan to whip the cream; be sure the cream itself is well-chilled (but don't put the cream in the freezer; if it starts to freeze, it won't make as good a foam).

Don't add sugar until you're almost through whipping. Added at the beginning, sugar decreases the final volume of the whipped cream.

Finally, stop beating when soft peaks form. Don't overbeat or you'll find yourself making butter.

RULE BRITANNIA

A Feast of Lamb

★

Meat, Centre-Stage

★

Dickensian Vegetables

★

Marvellous Muffins and Scones

★

Basically Bread

Until about 20 years ago, the West Coast kitchen sailed under a British flag. Roast beef and Yorkshire pudding or dripping on toast: food was simple, plain, filling and, it must be admitted, a tad overcooked.

Because the values of British cooking pervaded home economics teaching until the end of the 1960s, generations of B.C. high-school girls went out to meet the future armed with the knowledge that meat and potatoes makes a real dinner, oatmeal porridge is a life-enhancing substance and a good grasp of the muffin method will take you far.

Although the test kitchen now ventures into more exotic waters, we still have a file of recipes that salute our Anglo-Saxon heritage. After all, we don't call it British Columbia for nothing.

★ ★ ★ ★ ★

A Feast of Lamb

Over the years we have printed what seems like an enormous number of excellent lamb recipes. This is partly because Pat Pederson, a home economist in our kitchen for 20 years, likes to cook family dinners, and Pat is British, and partial to lamb. (If lamb isn't part of your culinary background, cultivate a close relationship with a good butcher.)

Very few interesting lamb recipes have passed our kitchen without careful study; here are a few of the best.

Rosemary Roast Leg of Lamb with Orange Basting Sauce

Makes six to eight servings

If you have fallen out of the habit of cooking dinners centred on roasts, you may have forgotten how easy they are. A six-pound leg of lamb can look daunting. But all you have to do is flavor it and put it away in the oven, popping in every once in a while to say hello and anoint it with basting sauce. For this one, you cut slits in the roast and stuff them with a mixture of rosemary and fresh garlic, then baste the lamb with a sauce made from red wine and orange juice concentrate.

1 (5 to 6-pound or 2.5 to 3-kg) leg of lamb
2 garlic cloves, crushed
1 tablespoon (15 mL) paprika
1 tablespoon (15 mL) chopped fresh rosemary
2 teaspoons (10 mL) salt
½ teaspoon (2 mL) pepper

Orange Basting Sauce:

¼ cup (50 mL) butter or margarine
1 (178-mL) can frozen orange juice concentrate, thawed
¼ cup (50 mL) dry red wine

With a sharp knife, cut 12 slits in lamb. Combine garlic, paprika, rosemary, salt and pepper. Press a little of the garlic mixture into each slit. Place lamb in shallow roasting pan.

Roast lamb at 350 F (180 C), for 20 minutes per pound (40 minutes per kg) or until meat thermometer registers 150 F (65 C) for medium-rare.

While lamb is roasting, combine sauce ingredients in one-quart (1-L) saucepan and simmer, uncovered, for 15 minutes. After lamb has roasted one hour, baste frequently with sauce until meat is done.

Place lamb on heated platter and allow to stand in warm place for 15 minutes before slicing. Skim excess fat from pan juices and make gravy if desired. ★

Marmalade Sesame Roast Lamb

Makes eight to 10 servings

Here's a recipe for British lamb going colonial. Sweet-tart marmalade, soy sauce, ginger and sesame oil combine to make a marinade and basting sauce with a rich and complex flavor. If you don't use ground ginger often, it's worth checking to see if the powder in the bottle still tastes like ginger, or just like powder.

1 cup (250 mL) Seville orange marmalade
2 tablespoons (30 mL) soy sauce
2 tablespoons (30 mL) sesame oil
2 garlic cloves, crushed
1 teaspoon (5 mL) ground ginger
2 teaspoons (10 mL) sesame seeds
1 (5-pound or 2.5-kg) boneless leg of lamb (not rolled)

In small bowl, combine marmalade, soy sauce, sesame oil, garlic, ginger and sesame seeds; set aside.

Trim any excess fat from lamb. Place lamb in large plastic bag and add marmalade mixture. Seal bag tightly and refrigerate at least eight hours or overnight, turning occasionally. Remove lamb from marinade; reserve marinade. Roll lamb up and tie at 2-inch (5-cm) intervals with string. Place lamb in roasting pan and pour one-half of the marinade around meat.

Roast lamb at 450 F (230 C) for 10 minutes, then lower heat to 350 F (180 C) for one to 1½ hours or until meat thermometer registers 150 F (65 C) for medium-rare, basting occasionally with remaining marinade. Let lamb stand for five to 10 minutes, loosely covered, before carving. ★

GROW YOUR OWN ROSEMARY

Every rosemary I have ever brought inside for the winter has dropped its leaves and died. Last year I bought a trailing rosemary, reputed to be hardier than most varieties, and, when winter came, sunk the pot in the sunniest spot in the garden. It lived.

Rosemary needs full sun and good air circulation – its enemies include moulds and fungi. It needs well-drained, but not rich soil.

Rosemary is a strong herb; you need cut only small amounts at a time for kitchen use. Cut from the new growth only. Cutting into woody parts will hinder the plant's development.

Lamb Chops with Sun-Dried Tomatoes

Makes four servings

Rosemary and lamb go together like turkey and sage. In this recipe lamb chops, quickly cooked, are kept warm while the cook makes a sauce with rosemary, red wine and sun-dried tomatoes.

Served with pasta or gnocchi and a green salad, this is the perfect supper for Friday nights, when you need a very quick, very good meal to celebrate the beginning of the weekend.

4 loin lamb chops, about 1½-inches (4-cm) thick
Freshly ground pepper to taste
¼ cup (50 mL) sun-dried tomatoes (packed in oil)
2 tablespoons (30 mL) olive oil
1 teaspoon (5 mL) finely chopped garlic
1 cup (250 mL) dry red wine
1 teaspoon (5 mL) dried rosemary, crushed

Sprinkle chops with pepper. Sliver sun-dried tomatoes; set aside.

Heat olive oil in frypan over medium-high heat. Add garlic and brown lightly; remove garlic and discard. Place chops in frypan and brown lightly on each side. Reduce heat, cover and cook for five minutes per side or until done. Remove chops and keep warm. Pour off all but one tablespoon (15 mL) fat from frypan.

Add wine, sun-dried tomatoes and rosemary to frypan. Cook until liquid is reduced by half, stirring occasionally. Pour sauce over chops. ★

WINE AND DINE

When a recipe in this book calls for wine, we mean a drinkable table wine, not the heavily salted cooking wines sold in grocery stores.

How do you decide which wine to use in cooking? The easiest way is to choose the wine you'll be drinking when the dish shows up at dinner.

If you don't drink wine and don't want to buy a full bottle to use only a cup, check the liquor store for wine in 375 mL bottles.

Mustard-Herb Grilled Lamb Chops

Makes four servings

Lamb chops are an easy dish for entertaining. These ones rest in a mustard, rosemary and thyme marinade for half an hour while you put together the vegetables. Then they get a quick searing, either outdoors on the grill or indoors under the broiler. In the summer, serve with corn, fresh tomatoes and potato salad. For the winter, start with a creamy soup, then serve with roasted yams.

- **12 small loin lamb chops**
- **1½ teaspoons (7 mL) chopped fresh thyme**
- **1½ teaspoons (7 mL) chopped fresh rosemary**
- **2 garlic cloves, crushed**
- **2 tablespoons (30 mL) Dijon mustard**
- **¼ cup (50 mL) soy sauce**
- **2 tablespoons (30 mL) vegetable oil**

Pat chops with paper towels to dry well.

Slash edges of chops and place in shallow baking dish. Sprinkle with thyme, rosemary and garlic, then spread with mustard.

Combine soy sauce and oil; pour over chops. Cover and let stand at room temperature for 30 minutes, turning occasionally. Or refrigerate for up to eight hours then let stand at room temperature for 30 minutes before grilling.

Remove chops from marinade. Place on greased barbecue grill and cook for about four to five minutes each side for rare, turning once. ★

Lamb Chops with Chutney

Makes four servings

This recipe gives huge rewards for efforts so minimal it's possible to consider cooking it even after a long hard day in the world. The secret is the chutney, which you rub on the chops to give them instant complex flavor. After that there's nothing to do but coat them with bread crumbs and sling them into the oven. Then you have 25 minutes to take whatever restorative measures seem best and pull together the rest of the meal.

- **1 cup (250 mL) fresh bread crumbs**
- **½ teaspoon (2 mL) dried thyme, crumbled**
- **¼ teaspoon (1 mL) salt**
- **⅛ teaspoon (0.5 mL) pepper**
- **3 tablespoons (45 mL) mango chutney**
- **1 teaspoon (5 mL) lemon juice**
- **4 loin lamb chops, about 2-inches (5-cm) thick**

Combine bread crumbs, thyme, salt and pepper on plate.

Combine chutney and lemon juice; spread completely over each chop. Coat each chop with bread-crumb mixture and place on greased baking sheet. Bake at 450 F (230 C) for about 25 minutes or until done. ★

Pink Geranium Marinated Lamb

Makes eight to 10 servings

This is the best barbecued lamb I have ever tasted. It came to the kitchen from Ken and Sylvia Mounsey who ran the tiny Pink Geranium restaurant on Galiano Island, almost as famous for the difficulty of getting into it as it was for its food. The Mounseys kept the restaurant small, because that's what they could handle, and kept it open only when they weren't off travelling. They cooked good, straight-forward but inspired British food, like this lamb impregnated with fresh mint.

Ken Mounsey says the secret lies in getting all the fat off the meat. He uses a boning knife and a patient attitude. You can marinate the lamb for up to 48 hours to intensify the flavor.

1 (5-pound or 2.5-kg) leg of lamb, boned and butterflied
⅓ cup (75 mL) olive oil
⅓ cup (75 mL) fresh lemon juice
1 cup (250 mL) fresh mint leaves
3 tablespoons (45 mL) liquid honey
1 (2-inch or 5-cm) piece fresh ginger, peeled
4 garlic cloves, peeled

Trim all fat from lamb.

In blender, combine oil, lemon juice, mint leaves, honey, ginger and garlic; blend until smooth. Place lamb and marinade in plastic bag; seal tightly. Marinate overnight in the refrigerator.

Remove lamb from the marinade and place on broiler pan. Broil 15 minutes on each side or until medium-rare. Slice thin to serve. ★

GROW YOUR OWN MINT

Mint is a hardy perennial that will gladly take over the garden if you let it. Plant it in pots to contain its root system. It likes a shady spot with moist, rich soil, but isn't all that fussy about where it grows.

Peppery peppermint makes the best herbal tea. Use it as an accent in iced drinks and salads.

Milder spearmint is the mint of choice for adding to peas, carrots and new potatoes.

Meat, Centre-Stage

Yes we do eat meat other than lamb. We may be eating a little less of it, we may eat it less often than we used to. But we still value the ease and speed of a meal that's anchored to a pork chop, and the drama of a prime rib roast dinner. We can be enchanted by pork tenderloin served with a port-laced fig coulis, but we still have space for a sticky '60s survivor like spare ribs cooked in a culinarily incorrect but still delicious dark rum sauce with ketchup.

Pork Chops with Balsamic Vinegar

Makes four servings

Nothing could be simpler than these quickly fried chops. Once they're cooked, add chicken stock and a dash of balsamic vinegar to the frypan to make a surprisingly complex tasting sweet-tart sauce.

- **4 single loin pork chops, about ¾-inch (2-cm) thick**
- **Freshly ground pepper**
- **2 teaspoons (10 mL) vegetable oil**
- **½ cup (125 mL) chicken stock**
- **1 tablespoon (15 mL) balsamic vinegar**

Sprinkle chops with pepper.

Heat oil in heavy frypan over medium-high heat. Add chops and cook for four to five minutes on each side or until done. Remove chops and keep warm.

Add stock and vinegar to frypan; cook until liquid is reduced to three tablespoons (45 mL), stirring constantly. Spoon sauce over chops. ★

Pork Chops with Parmesan and Fines Herbes

Makes four servings

Pound the chops to make them cook faster – the thick edge of a cleaver's blade will do if you don't have a meat mallet – and then dip them in flavored bread crumbs and cook them.

4 boneless butterfly centre cut pork chops
¼ cup (50 mL) fine dry bread crumbs
1 teaspoon (5 mL) fines herbes
¼ teaspoon (1 mL) salt
Pinch freshly ground pepper
¼ cup (50 mL) freshly grated parmesan cheese
1 egg
1 tablespoon (15 mL) water
1 tablespoon (15 mL) butter or margarine
1 tablespoon (15 mL) vegetable oil

Place chops between two sheets of plastic wrap and pound with a meat mallet until ¼-inch (5-mm) thick. Combine bread crumbs, fines herbes, salt, pepper and parmesan cheese. In small bowl, lightly beat egg and water together.

Dip each pork chop into egg mixture, then coat thoroughly with bread crumb mixture.

In frypan, heat butter and oil. Add chops and cook about four minutes on each side or until done. ★

PURE PARMESAN

I grew up thinking that parmesan cheese was a strong-tasting, salty, orange powder that you sprinkled out of a green tube onto anything you wanted to make more salty or more orange.

Authentic parmesan, with its rich, sharp flavor and crumbly texture, is another cheese entirely. You can recognize it by the lofty price and by the words "Parmigiano-Reggiano" – the name of the region of Italy where parmesan originated – stenciled on the rind.

Less expensive and less authentic parmesans can still be very pleasant. And, domestic or imported, any freshly grated parmesan puts the pre-grated cheese you find in supermarket deli sections to shame.

Store parmesan tightly wrapped in the refrigerator and grate it as you need it. You'll be amazed at the difference.

Pork Chops with Mustard and Cream

Makes four servings

Aided and abetted by the pan juices, you can make a very satisfying, very simple sauce, with grainy mustard, white wine and whipping cream.

4 single loin pork chops, about ¾-inch (2-cm) thick
½ teaspoon (2 mL) salt
¼ teaspoon (1 mL) pepper
1 tablespoon (15 mL) vegetable oil
2 tablespoons (30 mL) grainy mustard
3 tablespoons (45 mL) dry white wine
⅓ cup (75 mL) whipping cream

Sprinkle chops with salt and pepper.

Heat oil in large frypan. Add chops and cook for four to five minutes on each side or until done. Remove chops and keep warm.

Add mustard and wine to frypan; cook about one minute or until liquid is slightly reduced, stirring constantly. Stir in cream and simmer until slightly thickened, about two minutes. Pour sauce over chops. ★

Doug's Fiery Mediterranean Pork

Makes eight servings

This recipe from reader Doug Deans, a skiing, fly-fishing and cooking enthusiast, came to us as part of a story on men in the kitchen. Doug loves hot food, and his pork roast, marinated overnight in a spicy paste that includes two full heads of garlic, breathes fire.

Think of this recipe as an easy one for a dinner party: just put the meat in the marinade the night before, and time will help you out. Once you put the roast in the oven, you have two hours to get the rest of dinner ready.

- **2 heads garlic (about 20 cloves), separated into cloves and peeled**
- **¼ cup (50 mL) chopped fresh rosemary OR 2½ tablespoons (37 mL) dried**
- **2 teaspoons (10 mL) salt**
- **2 tablespoons (30 mL) freshly ground black pepper**
- **1½ teaspoons (7 mL) dried crushed chilies**
- **¼ cup (50 mL) olive oil**
- **1 (5-pound or 2.5-kg) bone-in pork loin roast**

In blender or food processor, process garlic, rosemary, salt, pepper and crushed chilies until well combined. With motor running, slowly pour in oil until well blended.

Place pork, bone-side down, in roasting pan. Coat with garlic mixture. Cover and place in refrigerator overnight.

Roast at 400 F (200 C) for 15 minutes, then reduce oven temperature to 325 F (160 C) and continue to roast for 1½ hours or until meat thermometer inserted in thickest part of pork (not touching bone) registers 170 F (75 C).

Place pork on heated platter and let stand 20 to 30 minutes. Pour off some of the fat and make gravy with remaining pan drippings. ★

Pork Tenderloin with Fig Coulis

Makes six to eight servings

One December we asked some city caterers what they'd serve at a sit-down dinner party for eight. This recipe was Lesley Stowe's answer: pork tenderloin with figs that have been soaked in brandy, pureed, enriched with butter and stirred into a cream sauce that incorporates the pan juices from the pork. You don't have to restrict this dish to December; it would be good for any lavish occasion.

- **6 dried figs, stems removed**
- **¼ cup (50 mL) port**
- **8 tablespoons (120 mL) unsalted butter, divided**
- **3 tablespoons (45 mL) water**
- **3 pounds (1.5 kg) whole pork tenderloins**
- **3 tablespoons (45 mL) red wine vinegar**
- **2 tablespoons (30 mL) finely chopped shallots**
- **1½ cups (375 mL) whipping cream**
- **Salt and freshly ground pepper to taste**

Cut figs into eighths and cover with port. Let marinate for one hour.

In saucepan, place two tablespoons (30 mL) butter, water and figs with port. Cover and simmer until figs are tender and most of the liquid has evaporated, 15 to 20 minutes. Puree fig mixture in food processor with two tablespoons (30 mL) butter.

In large frypan, melt three tablespoons (45 mL) butter. Add pork tenderloins and brown on all sides. Place tenderloins in roasting pan and roast at 375 F (190 C) for 18 to 25 minutes or until done.

Meanwhile, add vinegar, shallots and remaining one tablespoon (15 mL) butter to drippings in frypan. Bring to a boil, stirring constantly and scraping brown bits from bottom of pan. Add cream and cook until reduced by one-quarter. Add fig mixture and whisk. Season with salt and pepper.

To serve, slice tenderloins and place on warm dinner plates. Nap the sauce along one side of meat. ★

BUTTER UP

Because unsalted butter is just that – unsalted – it's more perishable than butters with added salt. Store it in the freezer, well-wrapped so it doesn't pick up off odors.

Rum Ribs

Makes five or six servings

Much as we love the barbecue, it won't do for sticky ribs like these. Baked in the oven, basted with a brown sugar and dark rum sauce, they're spicy and succulent.

4 pounds (2 kg) pork spareribs
1 cup (250 mL) brown sugar
½ cup (125 mL) chili sauce
¼ cup (50 mL) ketchup
½ cup (125 mL) dark rum
¼ cup (50 mL) soy sauce
1 tablespoon (15 mL) Worcestershire sauce
1 teaspoon (5 mL) dry mustard
2 garlic cloves, crushed
⅛ teaspoon (0.5 mL) pepper

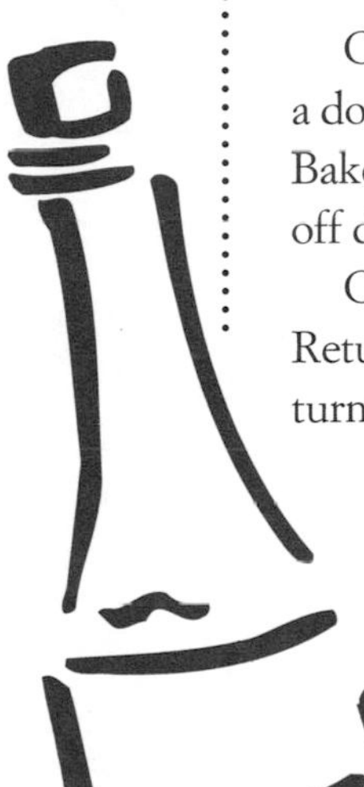

Cut spareribs into individual pieces. Line a roasting pan with a double thickness of foil. Place ribs in pan and seal tightly in foil. Bake at 350 F (180 C) for 45 minutes. Unwrap ribs and pour off drippings.

Combine remaining ingredients; pour half the sauce over ribs. Return to oven and bake for about 1½ hours or until meat is tender, turning ribs occasionally and basting with remaining sauce. ★

Honey Beef and Lentils

Makes four to five servings

This is an everyday sort of dish, a highly nutritious, inexpensive, low-fat main course that tastes far better than it should with that string of attributes. Reader Judy Jones, a teaching assistant who works with special-needs children in Burnaby, entered it in our ground beef recipe contest; it's especially useful to cooks who are trying to sell lentils to a less than entranced audience.

- 1⅓ **cups (325 mL) green lentils, rinsed**
- 1 **small bay leaf**
- 3 **cups (750 mL) water, divided**
- 1 **teaspoon (5 mL) salt**
- ½ **cup (125 mL) chopped onions**
- ½ **cup (125 mL) chopped celery**
- 2 **teaspoons (10 mL) vegetable oil**
- ½ **pound (250 g) lean ground beef**
- 1 **teaspoon (5 mL) dry mustard**
- ¼ **teaspoon (1 mL) ground ginger**
- 1 **tablespoon (15 mL) soy sauce**
- ¼ **cup (50 mL) liquid honey**

In large saucepan, combine lentils, bay leaf, 2½ cups (625 mL) water and salt; bring to a boil. Cover tightly, reduce heat and simmer for 30 minutes or until lentils are soft. Remove bay leaf but do not drain.

Meanwhile, saute onions and celery in oil in frypan until soft. Add beef and cook over low heat until browned; drain off fat and moisture.

In separate bowl, combine mustard, ginger, soy sauce and remaining ½ cup (125 mL) water. Add to lentils along with beef mixture. Place in six-cup (1.5-L) casserole. Top with honey and stir in. Cover tightly and bake at 350 F (180 C) for one hour, uncovering during last 10 minutes. ★

Roast Prime Rib with Cabernet Pan Sauce

Serves eight with leftovers

The fact that we cooked this standing rib roast as part of a Victorian Christmas dinner is, I suppose, some measure of how much our dinner tables have changed since the days when roast beef was close to synonymous with Sunday dinner. Our concession to current culinary trends is the cabernet sauce, much lighter than traditional gravies.

3 tablespoons (45 mL) coarse (pickling) salt
1 tablespoon (15 mL) freshly ground pepper
2 garlic cloves, chopped fine
1 (5-rib) prime rib of beef (about 9 pounds or 4 kg)
3 carrots, chopped coarse
3 celery stalks, chopped coarse
2 parsnips, chopped coarse
1 onion, chopped coarse
4 sprigs fresh thyme
3 bay leaves
Cabernet Pan Sauce (see recipe)

Combine coarse salt, pepper and garlic; rub mixture all over meat.

Spread vegetables, thyme and bay leaves in bottom of roasting pan and place meat on top. Roast at 350 F (180 C) for about 2½ hours. After one hour, baste frequently with pan drippings. For rare roast beef, remove meat from oven when meat thermometer registers 130 F (55 C) and let rest for 30 minutes before serving. Meanwhile, prepare cabernet pan sauce. ★

CABERNET PAN SAUCE

1 small onion, chopped fine
1 small carrot, chopped fine
1 celery stalk, chopped fine
5 whole black peppercorns
1 bay leaf
1 sprig fresh thyme
1 garlic clove, chopped fine
2 cups (500 mL) cabernet sauvignon wine
2 cups (500 mL) beef stock
Salt to taste

While meat rests, make the sauce. Discard cooked vegetables from roasting pan and pour off all but a tablespoon (15 mL) or so of the pan drippings. Add the raw onion, carrot and celery; place pan over medium to high heat and saute until vegetables are lightly browned, three to five minutes.

Add peppercorns, bay leaf, thyme and garlic to pan; saute for another two minutes. Add wine; stir and scrape brown bits from bottom of pan.

Add stock and bring to a boil, continue boiling until liquid is reduced by half, about 15 to 20 minutes. Season with salt, strain and transfer to sauce boat.

★ ★ ★ ★ ★

Dickensian Vegetables

Don't be looking for any stir-fried, just barely cooked green beans in this collection of recipes. These are vegetables with heft, suitable for use as side dishes at family feasts, or as the centrepiece of cold weather vegetarian meals. Okay, so Charles Dickens may never have eaten beets with ginger. But we bet he'd have liked them and, like all of these recipes, they'd go very well with a fat goose.

Fruity Glazed Brussels Sprouts and Onions with Chestnuts

Makes six servings

Chestnuts are fiddly to prepare, so we don't cook them often. Which means, of course, when they do get to the table, they look like exotic, special occasion food. They're even more exotic combined with brussels sprouts, onions and apricots cooked in a little caramelized brown sugar and then topped with rosemary and thyme.

12 fresh chestnuts
18 small white pearl onions
12 brussels sprouts, trimmed
3 tablespoons (45 mL) butter or margarine, divided
2 tablespoons (30 mL) dark brown sugar, divided
12 canned apricot halves, drained
1 teaspoon (5 mL) crumbled dried rosemary
½ teaspoon (2 mL) dried thyme
Salt and freshly ground pepper to taste

Cut a small X into the flat side of each chestnut, cutting through the woody outer shell; try not to cut into the meat. Place chestnuts in saucepan with enough boiling water to cover. Reduce heat and simmer for 20 to 30 minutes or until chestnuts are tender. Remove chestnuts from the water, one at a time. Peel off shell and thin brown skin; set aside.

Bring two quarts (2 L) water to a boil in large saucepan. Cut a small X in the root end of each onion and drop the onions into the water. Reduce heat and simmer until tender but firm, about eight to 10 minutes. Drain, rinse under cold water; drain again. Peel and set aside.

Bring another two quarts (2 L) of water to a boil. Cut a small X in the root end of each brussels sprout. Drop sprouts into water.

Reduce heat and simmer for about 10 minutes or until tender-crisp. With slotted spoon, remove sprouts, rinse under cold water and drain. Set aside.

Melt one tablespoon (15 mL) butter in frypan. Add reserved onions and sprinkle with one tablespoon (15 mL) brown sugar. Cook over medium-high heat for about three minutes or until caramelized, stirring frequently. With slotted spoon, remove onions from frypan; set aside.

Add one tablespoon (15 mL) butter to frypan. Add brussels sprouts and sprinkle with remaining one tablespoon (15 mL) brown sugar. Cook about three minutes or until caramelized, stirring frequently.

In 11x7-inch (28x17.5-cm) baking dish, arrange onions, brussels sprouts, apricots and chestnuts crosswise in rows of six, beginning and ending with onions. Dot with remaining one tablespoon (15 mL) butter and sprinkle with rosemary, thyme and salt and pepper. Bake at 350 F (180 C) for 15 to 20 minutes or until vegetables are tender and heated through. ★

BEET RED

Some cooks shy away from beets because of the color problem – uncontrollable dark purple beet juice that stains everything it touches.

The solution: common table salt. Rub it on newly purple hands and kitchen counters and the color lifts so quickly and completely that it's nothing short of magical.

Ginger Beets

Makes six servings

One of the best ways to eat beets is cooked, peeled, doused in oil and vinegar, sprinkled with salt and pebbled with as much raw garlic as you think decent. Ginger beets offer a more refined approach.

- **2 pounds (1 kg) medium beets**
- **½ cup (125 mL) raisins**
- **2 tablespoons (30 mL) butter or margarine**
- **1 tablespoon (15 mL) finely chopped fresh ginger**
- **1 tablespoon (15 mL) sugar**
- **1 teaspoon (5 mL) red wine vinegar**
- **2 teaspoons (10 mL) finely grated lime rind**

Trim stems from beets, leaving about 1 inch (2.5 cm) of stem on each; scrub under cold running water. Cook beets in boiling salted water in saucepan for 30 to 40 minutes or until tender; drain. Rinse with cold water and slip off skins. Slice beets and set aside.

Soak raisins in hot water for five minutes; drain.

Melt butter in large frypan over medium-high heat. Stir in ginger and cook for one minute, stirring constantly. Stir in raisins, sugar and vinegar. Add beets and cook until warmed through, stirring frequently. Place on platter and sprinkle with lime rind. ★

Braised Red Cabbage with Chestnuts

Makes six to eight servings

Roasted chestnuts, stewed gently in red cabbage and beef broth, make a depths-of-winter vegetable dish that best suits a rainy night, a fire in the fireplace and a table set with roast goose or pork.

30 fresh chestnuts
1½ pounds (750 g) red cabbage, sliced thin
¼ cup (50 mL) vegetable oil
¾ cup (175 mL) canned beef broth
¼ cup (50 mL) red wine vinegar
¼ teaspoon (1 mL) salt
Pinch freshly ground pepper
2 tablespoons (30 mL) sugar
2 tablespoons (30 mL) butter or margarine

Cut a small X into the flat side of each chestnut, cutting through the woody outer shell; try not to cut into the meat. Place chestnuts in single layer in baking pan and roast at 400 F (200 C) for 20 to 30 minutes or until tender. Peel off shells and thin brown skins. Coarsely chop chestnuts and set aside.

In large frypan, stir-fry cabbage in oil over medium-high heat for three minutes. Stir in broth, vinegar, chestnuts, salt and pepper. Bring to a boil. Reduce heat, cover and simmer for 10 minutes. Stir in sugar. Simmer, partially covered, for 20 to 30 minutes or until cabbage is tender and liquid has almost evaporated, stirring occasionally. Stir in butter. ★

HOW TO BUY CHESTNUTS

We once seriously considered banning chestnuts from the test kitchen because our purchases so often proved disappointing.

The chestnut ban didn't last, of course, and along the way we developed a few principles for picking them out.

· Price is no guarantee of quality.

· We've had better luck with European chestnuts, which show up in our stores late in October, than with the earlier imports from Asia.

· Look for a rich, dark mahogany color. The chestnuts should be glossy, plump and firm. Don't buy chestnuts that have air pockets under the shell.

· Italian specialty stores are a good source.

Scalloped Rutabaga and Apples

Makes eight servings

Sometimes you get surprises. "Microwaved rutabagas" is not, after all, the most encouraging answer to "What's for dinner?" But cut thin, gently spiced and mixed with equally thin slices of apple, this rutabaga dish turned out to be a Cinderella among turnips.

- **4 cups (1 L) thinly sliced peeled rutabaga (see note)**
- **4 cups (1 L) thinly sliced peeled apple**
- **1 teaspoon (5 mL) salt**
- **Pinch freshly ground pepper**
- **½ teaspoon (2 mL) ground nutmeg**
- **⅓ cup (75 mL) brown sugar**
- **2 tablespoons (30 mL) butter or margarine**

In large bowl, combine rutabaga, apple, salt, pepper, nutmeg and brown sugar. Spread rutabaga mixture evenly in greased two-quart (2-L) shallow microwaveable baking dish. Dot with butter.

Cover baking dish with microwaveable plastic wrap, venting one corner. Microwave at HIGH (full power) for 16 to 20 minutes, stirring every four minutes, or until rutabaga is tender. Let stand, covered, for three minutes.

If you don't have a microwave oven the casserole can be baked, covered, at 325 F (160 C) until the rutabaga is tender. Allow at least an hour.

Note: Cut rutabaga in half lengthwise. Cut each half into 1-inch (2.5-cm) thick slices and peel. Cut each slice into 1-inch (2.5-cm) thick strips and slice thin. ★

Sweet Potato Casserole with Hazelnuts and Maple Syrup

Makes six to eight servings

Who said vegetables can't be voluptuous? Sweet potatoes dressed for a party with butter, brown sugar and hazelnuts certainly are. This recipe makes a luxurious vegetarian dinner, especially with wild rice, an exotic greens salad and a loaf of serious bread. It works equally well as a side dish for a festive dinner.

- **5 medium sweet potatoes**
- **½ cup (125 mL) butter or margarine, at room temperature**
- **¼ cup (50 mL) brown sugar**
- **2 large eggs**
- **½ teaspoon (2 mL) salt**
- **1 cup (250 mL) milk**
- **2 tablespoons (30 mL) maple syrup**
- **½ cup (125 mL) chopped hazelnuts, toasted**

Pierce sweet potatoes and place on paper towels in microwave oven. Microwave at HIGH (full power) for 15 to 18 minutes or until tender. When cool enough to handle, peel sweet potatoes and mash well. You should have about three cups (750 mL).

Place sweet potatoes, butter, sugar, eggs, salt and milk in large bowl; beat until very smooth. Place in greased two-quart (2-L) microwaveable casserole. Microwave at MEDIUM (half power) for three minutes; stir.

Combine maple syrup and hazelnuts and sprinkle over sweet potato mixture. Microwave at MEDIUM for five minutes or until heated through. ★

A YAM, WHAT A YAM

There you are in the produce section, looking at two tubers.

One is light yellow. When you cook it the flesh stays dry. It is, let's admit this, a bit boring. We usually, and correctly, call it a sweet potato. The other, the one we incorrectly call a yam, is a thrilling shade of deep orange and goes all moist and sweet on cooking.

Truth be told, they're both sweet potatoes, members of the Convolvulus family and native to tropical America.

True yams, very seldom seen here except in ethnic markets, are from a different botanical family. The main distinguishing feature is size: yams can readily grow to 40 or 50 pounds; 600 pound yams six feet long have been recorded.

Marvellous Muffins and Scones

One of the most appealing of our British ways is that we like a nice cup of tea, especially if there's something pleasant to eat with it. In pursuit of this epiphany, we have tested hundreds of recipes for muffins and scones over the past few years.

It's true that the muffins we make are the American, quick-bread sort, not yeasted English muffins. And the ancestors of our scones were griddle breads in Scots households. But that's the sort of thing you have to expect in the colonies.

On the assumption that you don't need any more ordinary muffin recipes, here are a few less common combinations, along with an indispensable low-fat muffin made with prune paste.

As for our scones, you may notice that all of the recipes use buttermilk. After years of study devoted to this subject, we've come to believe that the best ones always do.

Fig-Orange Muffins

Makes 12 muffins

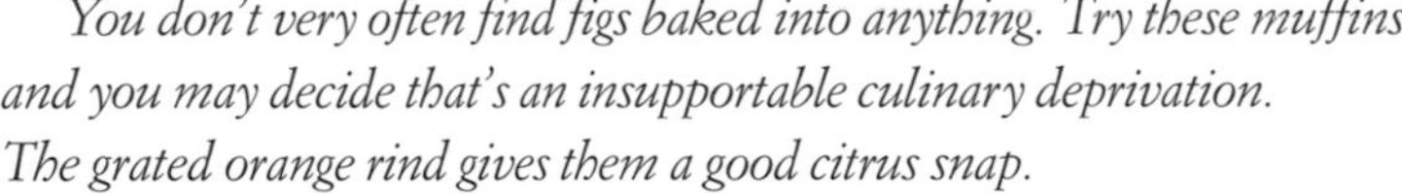

You don't very often find figs baked into anything. Try these muffins and you may decide that's an insupportable culinary deprivation. The grated orange rind gives them a good citrus snap.

- **2 cups (500 mL) all-purpose flour**
- **1 teaspoon (5 mL) baking soda**
- **½ teaspoon (2 mL) salt**
- **½ cup (125 mL) butter or margarine, at room temperature**
- **¾ cup (175 mL) sugar**
- **2 large eggs**
- **1 cup (250 mL) dried figs, cut up**
- **Grated rind of 1 orange**
- **1 cup (250 mL) plain yogurt**

In large bowl, combine flour, baking soda and salt. In another bowl, cream together butter and sugar. Add eggs to butter mixture and beat until fluffy.

Place figs and orange rind in food processor; process until mixture forms a paste. Blend fig paste into butter mixture; stir in yogurt. Add fig mixture all at once to flour mixture; stir just until dry ingredients are moistened.

Fill greased 3-inch (7-cm) muffin pans with batter. Bake at 400 F (200 C) for 15 to 17 minutes or until done. Remove muffins from pans and cool on wire rack. ★

★ ★ ★ ★ ★

Best Ever Bran Muffins: The Skinny Version

Makes 2½ dozen muffins

When prune paste substitutes for butter, the fat content drops from 9.66 grams per muffin in the original recipe to 0.83 of a gram per skinny muffin. Prune paste, made by whipping pitted prunes in a blender with a little water and vanilla, keeps the muffins moist. Oddly enough, you can't taste the prunes.

- **1 cup (250 mL) prune paste (see recipe)**
- **1½ cups (375 mL) packed brown sugar**
- **2 large eggs, well beaten**
- **2 tablespoons (30 mL) table molasses**
- **2¾ cups (675 mL) all-purpose flour**
- **1½ cups (375 mL) wheat bran**
- **2 teaspoons (10 mL) baking powder**
- **¼ teaspoon (1 mL) salt**
- **1 cup (250 mL) raisins**
- **2 teaspoons (10 mL) baking soda**
- **2 cups (500 mL) buttermilk**

In large bowl, beat together prune paste and sugar. Beat in eggs and molasses.

In medium bowl, combine flour, bran, baking powder and salt; stir in raisins. Stir soda into buttermilk; add to prune paste mixture alternately with flour mixture, stirring just until combined.

Spoon batter into greased muffin pans. Bake at 375 F (190 C) for about 20 minutes. Remove muffins from pans and cool on wire rack. ★

PRUNE PASTE

Makes one cup (250 mL)

- **1 cup (250 mL) pitted prunes**
- **6 tablespoons (90 mL) water**
- **2 teaspoons (10 mL) vanilla**

In blender or food processor, combine prunes, water and vanilla; process to form a smooth paste. Store in the refrigerator if not being used immediately. It will keep several days.

Cranberry Maple Muffins

Makes 12 muffins

The tart little explosion of whole cranberries makes for an unusual muffin. This is an especially good recipe to keep in mind if you find yourself with frozen cranberries and no turkey dinner on the horizon.

1½ cups (375 mL) all-purpose flour
½ cup (125 mL) chopped walnuts
2 teaspoons (10 mL) baking powder
½ teaspoon (2 mL) salt
1½ cups (375 mL) fresh cranberries
1 cup (250 mL) sugar
2 large eggs
½ cup (125 mL) butter or margarine (at room temperature), cut into 4 pieces
½ cup (125 mL) buttermilk
1½ teaspoons (7 mL) maple flavoring

Generously grease and lightly flour 12 muffin pans.

Place flour, walnuts, baking powder and salt in food processor; process until nuts are coarsely chopped. Transfer to medium bowl. Place cranberries in food processor and process using on/off pulses until cranberries are coarsely chopped. Add to dry ingredients.

Place sugar and eggs in food processor; process for one minute, stopping once to scrape down sides of work bowl. Add butter and blend until smooth, about one minute. With machine running, pour buttermilk and maple flavoring through feed tube and mix 10 seconds. Add dry ingredients. Process using on/off pulses until mixture is just combined.

Fill muffin pans with batter. Bake at 375 F (190 C) for 25 to 30 minutes or until done. Let muffins stand for one minute in pans before removing to wire rack to cool. Serve warm or at room temperature. ★

★ ★ ★ ★ ★

Lemon Apricot Scones

Makes eight scones

Dried apricots taste like sunshine. Bake them into scones flavored with lemon rind and, with a cup of tea, they're the perfect antidote to a rainy afternoon.

I've made them with grated orange rind on a day when I didn't have any lemons, and they were nice that way too.

- **2 cups (500 mL) all-purpose flour**
- **3 tablespoons (45 mL) sugar**
- **1 teaspoon (5 mL) baking soda**
- **½ teaspoon (2 mL) salt**
- **½ cup (125 mL) cold butter or margarine**
- **½ cup (125 mL) chopped dried apricots**
- **2 teaspoons (10 mL) grated lemon rind**
- **2 large eggs, divided**
- **½ cup (125 mL) buttermilk**

In large bowl, combine flour, sugar, baking soda and salt. With pastry blender, cut in butter until mixture resembles coarse crumbs. Stir in apricots and lemon rind. In separate bowl, whisk one egg into buttermilk; stir into flour mixture to form a soft dough.

Turn dough out on to lightly floured surface and knead gently about 10 times. Pat dough into a circle about ¾-inch (2-cm) thick; cut into eight wedges. Place on ungreased baking sheet. Lightly beat remaining egg; brush on scones.

Bake at 400 F (200 C) for 10 to 12 minutes or until done. Let cool on wire rack. ★

EGG-XACTLY

All recipes in this cookbook use large eggs.

Sometimes the hens I patronize lay medium-sized eggs, and I find myself wanting to bake but unwilling to go to the corner store for large eggs.

Should you find yourself in this predicament, here's a rough rule of thumb. If a recipe calls for one large egg, one medium egg is your best bet. If the recipe calls for two large eggs, use three medium eggs.

Currant Apple Scones

Makes 12 scones

Because of the moisture added by the grated apple, this scone gets away with less than the usual amount of butter.

- **2 cups (500 mL) all-purpose flour**
- **3 tablespoons (45 mL) sugar**
- **2½ teaspoons (12 mL) baking powder**
- **½ teaspoon (2 mL) baking soda**
- **½ teaspoon (2 mL) salt**
- **¼ cup (50 mL) cold butter or margarine**
- **¾ cup (175 mL) grated peeled apple**
- **½ cup (125 mL) currants**
- **¾ cup (175 mL) buttermilk**

In large bowl, combine flour, sugar, baking powder, soda and salt. With a pastry blender, cut in butter until mixture resembles coarse crumbs. Add apple, currants and buttermilk; stir to form a soft dough.

Turn dough out on to lightly floured surface and knead gently about eight to 10 times. Divide dough in half. Pat each half into a 6-inch (15-cm) circle; cut each circle into six wedges. Place on greased baking sheet.

Bake at 425 F (220 C) for 15 minutes or until done. Let cool on wire rack. ★

Orange Almond Scones

Makes 12 scones

Oh, splendid the morning with coffee and orange juice and scones as good as these. The only fussy bit is chopping the almonds. You can make early morning scones even easier by measuring out the dry ingredients the night before.

- ½ **cup (125 mL) orange juice**
- ¼ **cup (50 mL) buttermilk**
- 1 **large egg**
- ¼ **teaspoon (1 mL) almond extract**
- 3 **cups (725 mL) all-purpose flour**
- 4 **teaspoons (20 mL) baking powder**
- ½ **teaspoon (2 mL) baking soda**
- ¼ **teaspoon (1 mL) salt**
- ½ **cup (125 mL) cold butter or margarine**
- ½ **cup (125 mL) sugar**
- ⅓ **cup (75 mL) finely chopped almonds**
- 1 **tablespoon (15 mL) grated orange rind**

In small bowl, combine orange juice, buttermilk, egg and almond extract; beat with a fork until smooth.

In large bowl, combine flour, baking powder, baking soda and salt. With pastry blender, cut in butter until mixture resembles fine crumbs. Add sugar, almonds and orange rind; toss to combine. Add orange juice mixture and stir with a fork to form a soft dough.

Turn dough out on to lightly floured surface and knead gently five or six times. Divide dough in half. Pat each half into a 6-inch (15-cm) circle. Cut into six wedges. Place on ungreased baking sheet.

Bake at 400 F (200 C) for about 18 to 20 minutes or until done. Cool on wire rack. ★

★ ★ ★ ★ ★

Basically Bread

We like to bake bread. We like eating home-made even more than we like baking it. Yes, in our private lives, we're as short of kitchen time as anyone else. But we've learned to tailor our baking to the time available. Fresh herb Irish soda bread can be mixed and baked in under an hour. Instant yeast makes yeast bread a short-term project – two hours or less – but when we've got time, we pull out one of the old favorites with traditional yeast, and settle into an afternoon of risings and punching downs.

Fresh Herb Soda Bread

Makes one loaf

Anyone who's trying to eat lots of grains, fruits and vegetables rapidly finds out how important bread is. With a good loaf of home-made bread, simple, low-on-the-food-chain meals can be sublime. That being so, it's wise to have a soda bread recipe up your sleeve, particularly this one. If you keep buttermilk in your fridge, and herbs in your garden, tender, herb-rich bread is never more than an hour away.

- **2 cups (500 mL) whole-wheat flour**
- **1½ cups (375 mL) all-purpose flour**
- **2 tablespoons (30 mL) brown sugar**
- **1 tablespoon (15 mL) baking powder**
- **1 teaspoon (5 mL) baking soda**
- **1 teaspoon (5 mL) salt**
- **1 tablespoon (15 mL) chopped fresh thyme**
- **1 tablespoon (15 mL) chopped fresh basil**
- **1 tablespoon (15 mL) chopped fresh oregano**
- **1½ cups (375 mL) buttermilk**
- **2 large eggs**
- **2 tablespoons (30 mL) vegetable oil**

In large bowl, combine flours, brown sugar, baking powder, baking soda, salt, thyme, basil and oregano. In another bowl, whisk together buttermilk, eggs and oil. Add to flour mixture and stir just until dry ingredients are moistened.

Turn dough out on to floured surface and knead gently about seven to 10 times or until smooth. Shape into an 8-inch (20-cm) round and place on lightly greased baking sheet. With sharp knife, slash top with an X about ½-inch (1-cm) deep.

Bake at 375 F (190 C) for about 35 to 40 minutes or until brown and crusty. ★

Honey Whole-Wheat Sunflower Seed Bread

Makes two loaves

If you've never made yeast bread before, this honey whole-wheat sunflower bread, a little sweet, a little crunchy, is a good place to start. It uses instant yeast, which means you can have the finished bread out of the oven in less than two hours. How do you know when the dough has had enough kneading? Touch it to your cheek: it should feel smooth on top, and slightly moist. As a backup, set a timer for 10 minutes; beginning bread-makers tend to quit too soon.

2½ cups (625 mL) all-purpose flour, divided
2½ cups (625 mL) whole-wheat flour
1 cup (250 mL) sunflower seeds
2 teaspoons (10 mL) salt
2 (8-g) packages instant yeast
1 cup (250 mL) milk
1 cup (250 mL) water
⅓ cup (75 mL) liquid honey
¼ cup (50 mL) butter or margarine
Melted butter or margarine

Reserve 1½ cups (375 mL) of the all-purpose flour.

In large bowl, combine remaining one cup (250 mL) all-purpose flour, whole-wheat flour, sunflower seeds, salt and yeast.

In saucepan, heat milk, water, honey and the ¼ cup (50 mL) butter until very warm (125 to 130 F or 52 to 55 C); stir into flour mixture. Mix in enough of the reserved all-purpose flour to make a soft dough.

Turn dough out on to lightly floured surface and knead about eight to 10 minutes or until smooth and elastic, adding additional flour as needed. Cover and let rest for 10 minutes.

Divide dough in half. Shape each piece into a loaf and place in greased 8½x4½-inch (21x11-cm) loaf pan. Cover and let rise in warm place until doubled in size, about 40 minutes.

Bake at 375 F (190 C) for 30 to 40 minutes or until loaves sound hollow when tapped on bottom, covering loosely with foil during last 10 minutes of baking. Remove from pans. Brush with melted butter and cool on wire rack. ★

FROZEN FLOUR

Whole-wheat flours spoil quickly at room temperature. The germ of the wheat – the part that's removed from white flours – contains oils which go rancid.

Buy your whole-wheat flour from a store that has a brisk turnover. Store whole-wheat flour, tightly wrapped, in the refrigerator or freezer.

All-purpose flour will keep at a cool room temperature for about six months. If your kitchen is consistently hotter than 70 F (21 C) you may have problems with bug infestations and mould.

Bessie Forster's Carrot-Raisin Bread

Makes two loaves

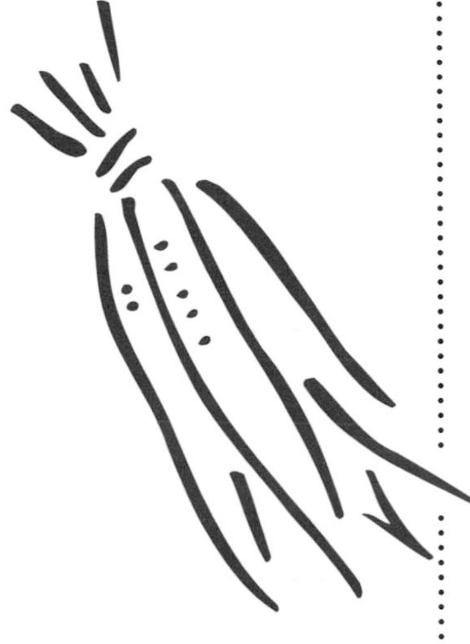

This recipe dates, as far as I know, from the '20s, when it was given to my grandmother by her neighbor, Bessie. We tested it last spring, and learned, to no one's surprise, that it still works beautifully.

1 teaspoon (5 mL) sugar
1 cup (250 mL) lukewarm water
1 (8-g) package traditional active dry yeast
1 cup (250 mL) milk, scalded
2 tablespoons (30 mL) sugar
1½ tablespoons (22 mL) butter or margarine
1½ teaspoons (7 mL) salt
1 large egg, beaten
6 to 6½ cups (1.5 to 1.625 L) all-purpose flour, divided
1 teaspoon (5 mL) ground cinnamon
¼ teaspoon (1 mL) ground allspice
¼ teaspoon (1 mL) ground cloves
2 cups (500 mL) grated raw carrots
1 cup (250 mL) raisins

Dissolve one teaspoon (5 mL) sugar in lukewarm water. Sprinkle yeast over and let stand in warm place for 10 minutes or until dissolved; stir.

In large bowl, combine milk, two tablespoons (30 mL) sugar, butter and salt; cool to lukewarm. Stir in egg and dissolved yeast.

Combine five cups (1.25 L) flour, cinnamon, allspice and cloves. Stir in grated carrots and raisins. Add to yeast mixture; stir well. Add enough of the remaining 1½ cups (375 mL) flour to form a soft dough.

Turn dough out on to lightly floured surface. Knead 10 minutes or until smooth and elastic, adding additional flour as needed. Place in greased bowl, turning to grease top. Cover and let rise in warm place until doubled in size, about one hour.

Punch dough down and divide in half. Shape each half into a loaf and place in greased 9x5-inch (23x12.5-cm) loaf pan. Cover and let rise in warm place until doubled in size, about 40 to 50 minutes.

Bake at 375 F (190 C) for 35 to 40 minutes or until loaves sound hollow when tapped on bottom. Remove loaves from pans and place on wire rack; brush tops lightly with butter if desired. ★

Cracked Pepper and Cheese Loaf

Makes two loaves

Grated old white cheddar and coarsely ground black pepper make this an unusual loaf. For one thing, it doesn't have the violent hues you can sometimes get from orange cheddar cheeses. Serve it with soup or chili, as a base for chicken sandwiches, or with a salad of bitter greens.

1 teaspoon (5 mL) sugar
1¼ cups (300 mL) lukewarm water
2 (8-g) packages traditional active dry yeast
1½ cups (375 mL) grated old white cheddar cheese
2 tablespoons (30 mL) sugar
1 tablespoon (15 mL) butter or margarine, at room temperature
1 teaspoon (5 mL) salt
1 teaspoon (5 mL) coarsely ground black pepper
3½ to 4 cups (875 to 1000 mL) all-purpose flour, divided
1 large egg, lightly beaten
1 egg white, lightly beaten
Coarsely ground black pepper

In large bowl, dissolve one teaspoon (5 mL) sugar in lukewarm water. Sprinkle yeast over and let stand in warm place for 10 minutes or until dissolved; stir.

Stir cheese, two tablespoons (30 mL) sugar, butter, salt, one teaspoon (5 mL) pepper and two cups (500 mL) of the flour into dissolved yeast. Add the one whole egg and enough of the remaining flour to make a soft dough.

Turn dough out on to lightly floured surface and knead for about four minutes or until smooth and elastic, adding additional flour as needed. Place in greased bowl, turning dough to grease top. Cover and let rise in warm place until doubled in size, about 30 minutes.

Divide dough in half. Shape each half into a loaf and place in greased 8½x4½-inch (21x11-cm) loaf pan. Cover and let rise in warm place until doubled in size, about 30 minutes.

Brush loaves with egg white. Sprinkle pepper along top of each loaf to make a lengthwise strip. Bake at 375 F (190 C) for 30 minutes or until loaves sound hollow when tapped on bottom. Remove from pans and cool on wire rack. ★

AS WHITE AS CHEDDAR CHEESE

Cheddar cheese is orange, right? Traditionally that's so, but only because cheesemakers added a natural dye called annatto – also used to color butter, margarine, other cheeses and smoked fish.

White cheddar can be just as flavorful as orange, and it makes delicious cheese bread.

Onion Rolls

Makes 12 rolls

Because they're leavened with instant yeast, these onion buns complete their two risings in under an hour. And because they're buns, they bake in 12 minutes. You can serve them with dinner, of course, but it's hard to imagine anything better for a grilled vegetable sandwich. We used instant minced onions in this bread because of their concentrated flavor.

3¾ to 4½ cups (925 to 1125 mL) all-purpose flour, divided
¼ cup (50 mL) sugar
2 (8-g) packages instant yeast
1½ tablespoons (22 mL) instant minced onion
2 teaspoons (10 mL) salt
¾ cup (175 mL) milk
½ cup (125 mL) water
3 tablespoons (45 mL) butter or margarine
3 large eggs, divided
Instant minced onion or poppy seeds

In large bowl, combine 1½ cups (375 mL) flour, sugar, yeast, 1½ tablespoons (22 mL) minced onion and salt.

In small saucepan, heat milk, water and butter until very warm (125 to 130 F or 50 to 55 C). Gradually add to flour mixture and beat two minutes at medium speed of electric mixer. Add two eggs and ½ cup (125 mL) flour. Beat at high speed for two minutes. Stir in enough of the remaining flour to make a soft dough.

Turn dough out on to lightly floured surface and knead for about four minutes or until smooth and elastic, adding additional flour as needed. Place dough in greased bowl, turning to grease top. Cover and let rise in warm place until doubled in size, about 30 minutes.

Punch dough down and divide into 12 pieces. Form each piece into a smooth ball. Place six balls on each of two greased baking sheets. Flatten balls with hand to about 3-inch (7-cm) rounds; cover.

Half-fill two large shallow baking pans with boiling water. Place baking sheets over pans. Let dough rise until doubled in size, about 20 minutes.

With sharp knife, cut ¼-inch (5-mm) deep X on top of each roll. Lightly beat remaining egg; brush on rolls. Sprinkle with instant minced onion or poppy seeds. Bake at 400 F (200 C) for 12 minutes or until done. Remove from baking sheets and cool on wire racks. ★

UBC Cinnamon Buns

Makes 18 large cinnamon buns

Cinnamon buns are hard to get right. Most people make them too sweet, or smother them in runny white icing. Not Grace Hasz, who contributed not just a bun but an entire culinary tradition to the University of B.C. when she pulled the first tray of these megabuns out of the oven in 1954. In the late '60s and early '70s, they blunted the sharp edges of many a winter morning for me. Now, 20 years later, I still take a cinnamon bun break if I find myself on campus early enough in the day. If you're having a nostalgia attack, here's the recipe. It makes a big batch.

Rolls:

- **3 cups (750 mL) milk**
- **6 tablespoons (90 mL) butter or margarine**
- **6 tablespoons (90 mL) sugar**
- **1 tablespoon (15 mL) salt**
- **1 teaspoon (5 mL) sugar**
- **½ cup (125 mL) lukewarm water**
- **2 (8-g) packages traditional active dry yeast**
- **2 large eggs**
- **9 cups (2.25 L) all-purpose flour, about**

Filling:

- **¾ cup (175 mL) melted butter or margarine, divided**
- **1¼ cups (300 mL) sugar**
- **2 tablespoons (30 mL) ground cinnamon**

For rolls: In saucepan, scald milk. Stir in butter, six tablespoons (90 mL) sugar and salt. Cool to lukewarm.

In small bowl, dissolve one teaspoon (5 mL) sugar in lukewarm water. Sprinkle yeast over and let stand in warm place for 10 minutes or until dissolved; stir.

In large bowl, combine lukewarm milk mixture and eggs. Stir in dissolved yeast. Add four to five cups (1 to 1.25 L) of the flour and beat well for 10 minutes. With wooden spoon, gradually add enough of the remaining flour to make a soft dough.

Turn dough out on to lightly floured surface and knead until smooth and elastic, about eight minutes, adding additional flour as needed. (This is a soft dough.) Place dough in greased bowl, turning to grease top. Cover with damp cloth and let rise in warm place until double in size, about one hour.

Punch down dough and turn out on lightly floured surface. Divide dough in half.

To fill, roll out each piece of dough into 9x18-inch (23x45-cm) rectangle. Brush each rectangle generously with some of the melted butter. Combine 1¼ cups (300 mL) sugar and cinnamon. Sprinkle an equal portion on each rectangle. Roll dough up like a jelly roll, starting from the long side. Cut into 2-inch (5-cm) slices.

Place remaining melted butter in bottom of 16½x11½x2½-inch (41x29x6-cm) baking pan. Arrange slices in pan and cover loosely with greased wax paper. Let rise until doubled in size, about 45 to 60 minutes.

Bake at 350 F (180 C) for 35 to 45 minutes. Remove from oven and immediately invert on to serving tray. ★

ON THE RIM

Salad for Dinner

★

Salads on the Side

★

Stir-Fries: From Classic to Adventurous

★

Putting the Rim on the Grill

★

A Duet of Noodle Recipes

★

Tropical Sweets

Back in the 1950s, Edith Adams Cottage published a series of booklets, including Home Preservation of Foods, Wedding Etiquette and Pressure Cookery. The one I'd dearly love to see was called: Foreign Foods.

What measures had to be taken, I wonder, to compress all the world's cuisines into one booklet? And what would its authors think if they could take a walk through Vancouver's Chinatown today?

You could write a booklet – or a book – on tropical fruits alone. But we get more than just pomelos, star fruit, rambutans and mangosteens. We also get hoisin sauce, soy sauce, fish sauce and miso paste. Perched on the edge of the Pacific, we face the Asian tropics and a dozen fragrant, sensually rich, highly evolved cuisines.

Perhaps in time we'll develop our own distinctive voice in the continuing food conversation, some blend of cuisines as rich as Nonya food in Singapore. For now, we're content to paddle on the Pacific shore, dazzled by the choices, playing with the flavors.

★ ★ ★ ★ ★

Salad for Dinner

Main-dish salads with a Pacific Rim flavor make perfect sense if you think about it: when it's hot, you feel like eating salad for dinner. The tropical parts of the Pacific Rim have applied themselves for centuries to satisfying the urge for something light, but filling, cool and crunchy, with enough spice to interest heat-flattened tastebuds. We're glad to have this tradition to borrow from.

Gado Gado

Makes six servings

One of the great glories of Indonesian food is peanut sauce. This one, with its chutney, chili peppers, garlic and coconut cream is especially rich and subtle. Gado Gado is a salad best made in the summer, when local vegetables are at their peak, but you can use the peanut sauce any time.

Peanut Sauce:

- ¼ **cup (50 mL) vegetable oil**
- 2 **garlic cloves, chopped fine**
- 1½ **cups (375 mL) finely chopped unsalted peanuts**
- 2 **tablespoons (30 mL) curry powder**
- ¼ **cup (50 mL) fruit chutney**
- 2 **small chili peppers, chopped fine**
- ¼ **cup (50 mL) lemon juice**
- 2 **tablespoons (30 mL) soy sauce**
- 1¼ **cups (300 mL) coconut cream**
- 1 **cup (250 mL) water**

Vegetables:

- 12 **small new potatoes**
- 1 **pound (500 g) broccoli, cut into small flowerets**
- 2 **carrots, peeled and cut into julienne strips**
- 3 **cups (750 mL) snow peas**
- 3 **cups (750 mL) bean sprouts**
- **Hard-cooked egg for garnish**

For peanut sauce: Place oil in saucepan over medium heat. Add garlic and peanuts; cook for two minutes, stirring constantly. Add curry powder, chutney and chili peppers; cook for another two minutes. Add lemon juice, soy sauce, coconut cream and water; cook over medium-low heat for 30 minutes, stirring occasionally to prevent sticking and burning.

Meanwhile, prepare vegetables: In saucepan, simmer potatoes in water over medium heat for 15 minutes or until tender; drain. In separate saucepans, cook broccoli and carrots in salted water until just tender; drain. Blanch snow peas in boiling water for one minute; drain. Arrange all the vegetables on a platter; garnish with sliced or quartered egg. Top with warm peanut sauce and serve immediately. ★

Chicken Pomelo Salad

Makes four servings

Pomelos look like the granddaddies of all grapefruits, and they are: botanists believe these giant, thick-skinned, citrus fruits are one of the grapefruit's ancestors. You can use them in almost any way you'd use a grapefruit, but if you get one of the sweet, deep-red-fleshed varieties, the effect is ever so much nicer. Try this salad with cooked crab meat or grilled prawns instead of chicken for a luxurious variation.

- **2 small whole chicken breasts, boned and halved**
- **Salt and freshly ground pepper to taste**
- **3 tablespoons (45 mL) lime juice**
- **2 tablespoons (30 mL) fish sauce (see note)**
- **1½ tablespoons (22 mL) brown sugar**
- **2 small garlic cloves, crushed**
- **2 small red chili peppers, seeded and sliced**
- **1 stem lemon grass, sliced thin**
- **1 bunch watercress, trimmed**
- **1 pomelo, peeled and sectioned**

Sprinkle chicken breasts with salt and pepper; place in baking pan.

Bake at 400 F (200 C) for 20 to 25 minutes or until cooked. Set aside to cool; cut into strips.

Combine lime juice, fish sauce, brown sugar, garlic, chili peppers and lemon grass. Stir in chicken strips.

Line each serving plate with watercress. Arrange an equal portion of pomelo sections on each plate; top with an equal portion of chicken mixture.

Note: Fish sauce, a salted and fermented sauce that's basic to several Pacific Rim cuisines, is available at Asian markets. ★

Peppery Chicken and Nectarine Salad with Lime

Makes four servings

Cook the chicken breasts the night before, and you can put this hot salad together in less than an hour. Much of its appeal comes from contrasts: acid lime juice against sweet ripe nectarines, hot pepper against cool lettuce. Serve it as a spur to jaded summer appetites.

2 small whole chicken breasts, cooked, boned and skinned
1 cup (250 mL) chopped onions
2 tablespoons (30 mL) vegetable oil
1½ teaspoons (7 mL) finely chopped garlic
¼ teaspoon (1 mL) crushed dried hot red pepper
½ teaspoon (2 mL) ground cumin
2 tablespoons (30 mL) soy sauce
1 red bell pepper, cut into thin strips
3 nectarines, cut into wedges
1 tablespoon (15 mL) fresh lime juice
Lettuce
Lime twists

Cut chicken into strips; set aside.

In large frypan, saute onions in oil until tender, about three minutes. Add garlic, hot red pepper, cumin, soy sauce, red bell pepper, nectarines and chicken; heat through, about three minutes. Sprinkle lime juice over top.

Serve hot salad on lettuce-lined platter. Garnish with lime twists. ★

Warm Seafood and Pineapple Salad with Basil-Mustard Sauce

Makes four servings

Okay, this is fancy food: Italy meets the Pacific Rim with a little tropical fruit thrown in. It's also pretty to look at, and easy to make. Once the fish and the pineapple spears are marinating, there's not a whole lot to do before dinner but weigh the merits of Italian white wine against some crisp dry beer – there's chutney in the salad, after all.

Basil-Mustard Sauce:

- ½ teaspoon (2 mL) prepared mustard
- ½ teaspoon (2 mL) Dijon mustard
- 1½ teaspoons (7 mL) chopped fresh basil
- 1 teaspoon (5 mL) drained capers
- ½ cup (125 mL) mayonnaise

Salad:

- 1 medium pineapple
- 3 tablespoons (45 mL) mango chutney, divided
- 4 teaspoons (20 mL) lemon juice, divided
- ½ teaspoon (2 mL) crushed garlic
- 2 tablespoons (30 mL) vegetable oil, divided
- ¾ pound (375 g) cod fish, cut into 1½-inch (4-cm) chunks
- 8 large shelled raw prawns
- ¼ cup (50 mL) chopped green onions
- 8 cherry tomatoes, halved
- Fresh basil sprigs for garnish

For sauce: In small bowl, blend mustards, basil, capers and mayonnaise. Cover and place in refrigerator while preparing salad.

For salad: Trim pineapple, quarter lengthwise and cut off core. Halve each quarter lengthwise to make eight spears. Combine two tablespoons (30 mL) chutney with two teaspoons (10 mL) lemon juice; drizzle over pineapple. Cover and refrigerate for one to two hours.

Combine remaining one tablespoon (15 mL) chutney, two teaspoons (10 mL) lemon juice, garlic and one tablespoon (15 mL) oil. Pour over cod and prawns. Cover and refrigerate for one to two hours.

To assemble salad: With slotted spoon, remove cod and prawns from marinade; reserve marinade. Heat remaining one tablespoon (15 mL) oil in frypan and stir-fry cod and prawns over medium-high heat until just cooked. Stir in onions and tomatoes along with reserved marinade and heat through.

With slotted spoon, remove fish mixture and place an equal portion in centre of each of four warm plates. Arrange a pineapple spear on each side of fish mixture; cut pineapple into 1-inch (2.5-cm) chunks. Top fish with a spoonful of mustard sauce. Garnish with basil sprigs. ★

MAYO CLINIC

I grew up thinking that the blue-and-white Miracle Whip salad dressing jar in the fridge held the same substance the rest of the world knew as mayonnaise.

Now I know that mayonnaise is something entirely different.

Technically, it's an emulsion of vegetable oil, lemon juice or vinegar, egg yolks and seasonings. Salad dressing doesn't contain any eggs and it's sweeter than mayonnaise. The taste difference is chalk and cheese. If you have a blender, an electric mixer or a food processor, you can make mayonnaise at home with minimal effort — and the taste and texture is better than anything you can buy.

The catch: home-made mayonnaise has a short life, three to four days in the refrigerator.

★ ★ ★ ★ ★

Warm Pork Tenderloin Salad with Honey Ginger Dressing

Makes four servings

When you are caught between the summer desire for every meal to be a salad and the longing for something more substantial, try this undeniably meaty recipe. The pork tenderloin marinates overnight.

Honey Ginger Dressing:

1 teaspoon (5 mL) finely chopped fresh ginger
3 tablespoons (45 mL) balsamic vinegar
1 teaspoon (5 mL) Dijon mustard
¼ cup (50 mL) vegetable oil
2 teaspoons (10 mL) liquid honey
¼ teaspoon (1 mL) salt
Pinch freshly ground pepper

Salad:

1 pound (500 g) pork tenderloin
1 garlic clove, crushed
2 teaspoons (10 mL) soy sauce
1 tablespoon (15 mL) sesame oil
¼ teaspoon (1 mL) freshly ground pepper
8 cups (2 L) torn mixed salad greens
1 red bell pepper, cut into strips
5 green onions, sliced
1 stalk celery, sliced diagonally

For dressing: In bowl, whisk together all dressing ingredients. (Dressing can be made a day ahead.)

For salad: Pound pork to ½-inch (1-cm) thickness. Combine garlic, soy sauce, sesame oil and pepper; brush on pork. Cover pork and place in refrigerator overnight.

Several hours before serving time, prepare vegetables and place in refrigerator.

To cook pork, place on broiler pan and broil 5 inches (12.5 cm) from heat for six to eight minutes or until done, turning once. Transfer meat to a plate and let rest for five minutes. Pour juices from broiler pan into the dressing; stir well.

Arrange salad greens on serving platter. Cut pork across the grain in thin slices and arrange over the lettuce. Sprinkle the red pepper, green onions and celery around the meat; drizzle with dressing. ★

SAVE YOUR GINGER

Wrap ginger tightly in plastic and store it in the fridge. It will keep several days. For longer storage, peel ginger, wrap in aluminum foil and freeze. When you need ginger, grate off the amount you need without thawing it.

Or peel ginger and immerse it in a jar of dry sherry. It will keep indefinitely in the fridge. The sherry has little impact on the ginger taste, but the ginger flavors the sherry. You can re-use the sherry for storing more ginger or add it as a secret ingredient to stir-fries and fruit salads.

★ ★ ★ ★ ★

SALADS ON THE SIDE

My favorite salad is made by drizzling arugula and baby lettuce leaves, fresh from the garden, with olive oil and balsamic vinegar and grinding on some pepper and salt. It's infinitely variable with the addition of sweet red peppers, olives, artichoke hearts, sun-dried tomatoes, fresh basil, or whatever the vegetable drawer contains. It's so simple there's no point in writing out a recipe.

For more orchestrated fare, two Pacific Rim salads stand out. Vietnamese Salad Rolls are salad in a wrapping, low in fat and fun to eat. The Strawberry and Avocado salad brings together several of my favorite flavors in one harmonious bowl.

Strawberry Avocado Salad

Makes four servings

When you like a particular taste a lot, it's hard to resist trying it out in every possible combination. One of the flavorings we use again and again is balsamic vinegar, and it's remarkable how often Brenda Thompson says: "Of course it tastes good. It's got balsamic vinegar in it." That's certainly true of this strawberry and avocado salad with water chestnuts and a shallot-spiked dressing. If you find fresh water chestnuts, peel them and slice them raw into the salad. You'll be astonished: it's like the difference between fresh and canned grapes.

Salad:

- **1 head romaine lettuce, torn into bite-size pieces**
- **1 avocado, seeded, peeled and sliced**
- **2 cups (500 mL) thickly sliced strawberries**
- **1 (227-mL) can sliced water chestnuts, drained**
- **½ cup (125 mL) pecan pieces**

Balsamic Dressing:

- **2 tablespoons (30 mL) balsamic vinegar**
- **1 tablespoon (15 mL) brown sugar**
- **6 tablespoons (90 mL) vegetable oil**
- **1 tablespoon (15 mL) finely chopped shallots**
- **Salt and freshly ground pepper to taste**

For salad: In large bowl, toss salad ingredients.

For dressing: In small bowl, whisk together vinegar and sugar. Gradually whisk in oil. Stir in shallots. Add salt and pepper. Add enough dressing to salad to coat lightly. ★

Vietnamese Salad Rolls

Makes 16 rolls

I discovered salad rolls when Granville Island Market opened. They're remarkably easy to make at home. Cram them with the nicest hand-peeled shrimp money can buy, or leave the shrimp out altogether and make a vegetarian version, adding half a cup of whatever suits your fancy.

- **2 ounces (60 g) rice vermicelli, about**
- **Hot water**
- **1 tablespoon (15 mL) vinegar**
- **16 sheets rice paper (about 9 inches or 23 cm in diameter)**
- **½ cup (125 mL) finely chopped green onions**
- **¾ cup (175 mL) grated carrots**
- **½ cup (125 mL) finely chopped celery**
- **½ cup (125 mL) finely chopped water chestnuts**
- **½ pound (250 g) cooked shrimp**
- **2 cups (500 mL) shredded lettuce**
- **Hot peanut sauce (see recipe)**

In large pot of boiling water, cook vermicelli about four to five minutes or until tender; drain. Rinse and drain well. Cut vermicelli in half for easier handling.

Fill large bowl with hot water; add vinegar. Place one sheet of rice paper in hot water until slightly soft. Carefully remove rice paper from water.

Place a small portion of noodles in centre of paper; add small portions of green onions, carrots, celery, water chestnuts, shrimp and lettuce. Fold the sides of the rice paper in and roll up. Place seam-side down on plate. Repeat with remaining rice paper and filling. If not served immediately, cover with a damp cloth and refrigerate. Serve with hot peanut sauce. ★

HOT PEANUT SAUCE

Makes about ½ cup (125 mL)

- **¼ cup (50 mL) peanut butter**
- **1 small red chili pepper, seeded and cut into pieces**
- **3 tablespoons (45 mL) soy sauce**
- **2 tablespoons (30 mL) water or coconut milk, about**

Place peanut butter, chili pepper and soy sauce in blender and process until well combined, adding water to give desired consistency. Place sauce in small saucepan; heat just until warmed through if desired.

Stir-Fries: From Classic to Adventurous

It's hard to remember life before woks. Stir-frying vegetables is second-nature to us now, and stir-fried dinners – meat and vegetables in one dish, rice to round it out – appear in our weekly fast cooking feature, Six O' Clock Solution, with a frequency matched only by pasta.

Some of the recipes here are as close to classic Chinese dishes as you'll find. Others are the kind of hybrid you get when a culinary technique goes travelling and settles down in a new spot. We like both kinds.

ASPARAGUS TIP

Before you cook asparagus, break off the woody end of the stalk. How far up the stalk is it woody? Never try to guess, and don't bother cutting it with a knife. Instead, let the asparagus give you the answer. Grasp the stem end in one hand, the tip in the other, and bend gently. The stalk will break at the point where the asparagus is tender enough for the table.

Chinese Asparagus

Makes four servings

Asparagus used to be one of the signs of spring here, that is until Mexican asparagus started appearing in the markets before the crocuses had bloomed. Whatever the time of year, it's especially good cooked in a wok in ginger-flavored oil.

- **1 pound (500 g) asparagus**
- **2 tablespoons (30 mL) vegetable oil**
- **6 slices unpeeled fresh ginger**
- **¼ teaspoon (1 mL) salt**
- **3 tablespoons (45 mL) chicken stock**
- **1 tablespoon (15 mL) soy sauce**
- **Toasted sesame seeds**

Snap off tough ends of asparagus. Cut asparagus diagonally into 2-inch (5-cm) pieces.

Heat large wok or heavy frypan over high heat. Add oil and heat.

Add ginger and toss for two to three minutes or until browned; remove and discard ginger. Add salt and asparagus to oil; cook for one minute. Add stock and soy sauce; cook for two to three minutes or until asparagus is tender-crisp. With slotted spoon, remove asparagus to platter. Sprinkle with sesame seeds. ★

Stir-Fried Vegetables with Oyster Sauce

Makes six servings

If vegetables always tasted this good, children would grow up clamoring for broccoli.

2 tablespoons (30 mL) vegetable oil
1 tablespoon (15 mL) finely chopped fresh ginger
3 cups (750 mL) broccoli flowerets
2 cups (500 mL) cauliflowerets
3 tablespoons (45 mL) chicken stock
1 cup (250 mL) sliced mushrooms
½ medium red or green bell pepper, cut into strips
1 tablespoon (15 mL) oyster sauce
1 teaspoon (5 mL) sesame oil

In wok, heat vegetable oil over high heat. Add ginger. As soon as it sizzles, add broccoli and cauliflower; stir-fry until vegetables are coated with oil. Add chicken stock; cover and cook for two minutes.

Add mushrooms and pepper strips; stir-fry one to two minutes or until vegetables are tender-crisp. Stir in oyster sauce and sesame oil. ★

PRAWN-OGRAPHY

To shell and devein prawns, start at the head end, dig in with your thumb by the legs, and the shell should slip off easily, with a gentle tug to get the sweet bit of tail meat free.

To devein, use a paring knife to cut in about ⅛-inch along the outer curve of the back, from the head to the tail, revealing the vein. Lift the vein out with the point of the paring knife. When you're done, rinse prawn under cold water.

To butterfly: peel the prawn, leaving on the tail. Cut from the underside, almost through to the vein, to make the hinge, open and flatten to form butterfly shape.

Garlic Prawns

Serves two as a main course
or four in combination with other dishes

In the test kitchen we like to promote the idea of the international pantry. Our premise: with a pantry full of the right oils, staples and seasonings, you can make the sort of fast, authentic food that a Chinese, Italian, Thai or Mexican cook would make at home. This recipe, from Tony Vong of Vong's Kitchen, was part of a story on the Chinese pantry. Vong suggests that, for the richest taste, you buy dry red peppers whole, and roast them in a dry wok before crushing them.

1 pound (500 g) raw tiger prawns in shell
2 tablespoons (30 mL) vegetable oil
3 garlic cloves, chopped fine
¼ to ½ teaspoon (1 to 2 mL) crushed dried chilies

Sauce:

2¼ teaspoons (11 mL) sugar
¾ teaspoon (4 mL) salt
1 teaspoon (5 mL) dark soy sauce
3 tablespoons (45 mL) water
2 teaspoons (10 mL) dry sherry

With scissors, trim off legs of prawns. With sharp knife, score back of prawns cutting through shell; devein prawns. Rinse with cold water and pat dry. Set aside.

Combine sauce ingredients and set aside.

Heat wok or frypan over high heat. Add oil and heat until oil starts to smoke lightly. Add garlic and chilies; brown lightly, stirring constantly.

Add prawns and cook for about two minutes, tossing to cook evenly. Pour in sauce mixture and stir well; cook another three minutes, stirring occasionally. ★

Fried Chili Crabs

Makes four servings

Stir-fried crab is one of the great Chinese-restaurant dishes, made more poignant by the inspection of the live crab before dinner. You can easily duplicate the same dish at home, without having to wave good-bye.

Don't boil live crabs. Instead, get the fishmonger to dispatch them with one quick blow on the edge of a sink. You get the mostly cleaned body broken in half. At home, clean off any remaining gills and crab butter. Cook the crab at once, or store it in the fridge for up to two hours.

This recipe for chili crabs, stir-fried in their shells, is spicy, but not punishingly hot.

2 medium raw crabs, cleaned
½ cup (125 mL) vegetable oil
2 teaspoons (10 mL) finely grated fresh ginger
3 garlic cloves, chopped fine
3 dried chilies, seeded and chopped
¼ cup (50 mL) tomato sauce
¼ cup (50 mL) chili sauce
1 tablespoon (15 mL) sugar
1 tablespoon (15 mL) light soy sauce
1 teaspoon (5 mL) salt

Cut each crab into four pieces. Heat oil in wok until very hot. Add crab pieces and fry until they change color, turning them to cook on all sides. Remove crab and set aside.

Remove wok from heat and immediately add ginger, garlic and chilies. Stir in tomato sauce, chili sauce, sugar, soy sauce and salt. Return wok to heat and bring tomato mixture to a boil. Add crab; cover and simmer for three minutes. Serve with rice if desired. ★

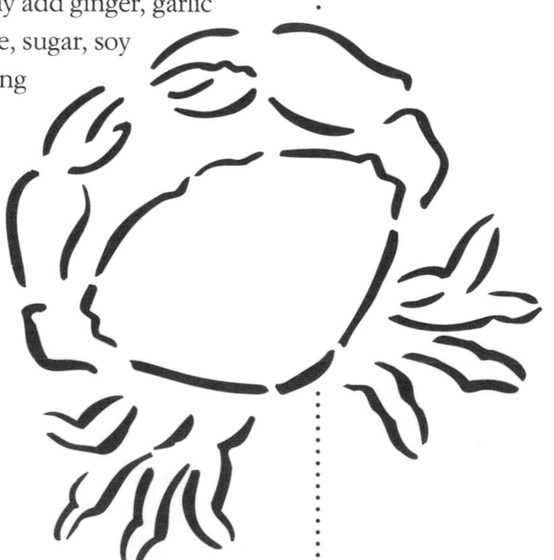

STOCK UP!

Whether you buy chicken stock or make your own, it's always worth freezing a cup or two in ice cube trays. Once you have stock cubes, store them in freezer bags. Then, when a stir-fry recipe calls for three tablespoons of chicken stock, all you have to do is melt a cube or two in the microwave.

Chicken and Bell Pepper Stir-Fry

Makes four servings

Fast, colorful, low in fat, delicious: how many virtues can one recipe have? This is the kind of stir-fry that has entered the vocabulary of West Coast cooks. It's so well suited to family meals that it no longer seems foreign in any way. Start the rice as soon as you get into the kitchen; after it's come to a boil and been turned down to simmer, start chopping the stir-fry ingredients.

2 whole chicken breasts, boned and skinned
¼ cup (50 mL) chicken stock
1 tablespoon (15 mL) soy sauce
2 teaspoons (10 mL) cornstarch
2 tablespoons (30 mL) vegetable oil
1 garlic clove, chopped fine
1 tablespoon (15 mL) finely chopped fresh ginger
1 small red bell pepper, cut into thin strips
1 small green bell pepper, cut into thin strips
4 green onions, cut into 1-inch (2.5-cm) pieces
Salt and freshly ground pepper to taste

Cut chicken into thin strips. Combine stock, soy sauce and cornstarch; set aside.

In wok, heat oil over high heat. Add garlic, ginger and chicken and stir-fry for about two minutes or until chicken is almost cooked. Add red and green bell peppers and green onions; stir-fry for one minute.

Pour stock mixture into frypan; cook for one minute or until slightly thickened and vegetables are tender-crisp. Season to taste with salt and pepper. ★

Szechuan-Style Chicken and Snow Pea Stir-Fry

Makes four servings

On the theory that there can never be too many recipes for good, fast suppers, here's another look at stir-fried chicken, this time with the peppery taste of Szechuan food.

Granted, it's not particularly authentic, since bottled Mexican picante sauce takes the place of dry hot red peppers. But it's a 20-minute meal, and it tastes great. Besides, who said Mexico wasn't part of the Pacific Rim?

2 small whole chicken breasts, boned and skinned
½ cup (125 mL) mild picante sauce
2 tablespoons (30 mL) soy sauce
1 tablespoon (15 mL) cornstarch
2 teaspoons (10 mL) grated fresh ginger
1½ teaspoons (7 mL) sugar
2 tablespoons (30 mL) vegetable oil, divided
2 large garlic cloves, chopped fine
1 red bell pepper, cut into short thin strips
1 cup (250 mL) pea pods, diagonally sliced in half
1 cup (250 mL) diagonally sliced green onions (¾-inch or 2-cm pieces)
Hot cooked rice, optional

Cut chicken into thin strips.

In small bowl, combine picante sauce, soy sauce, cornstarch, ginger and sugar; set aside.

In large frypan, heat one tablespoon (15 mL) of oil over medium-high heat. Add chicken and garlic; stir-fry two to three minutes or until cooked through. Remove chicken from frypan; set aside.

Add remaining one tablespoon (15 mL) oil to frypan. Add bell pepper and pea pods; stir-fry three minutes or until vegetables are tender. Stir picante sauce mixture; add to frypan with green onions and chicken. Cook and stir one minute or until sauce thickens. Serve with rice. ★

Pork Stir-Fry with Apples and Coriander

Makes four servings

Pork and apples are natural partners – as in roast pork and applesauce. Here they're paired in a less traditional but equally delicious way, abetted by sherry, soy sauce and ground coriander. A great dish for days when you don't have a lot of time, it's ready for the table in less than half an hour.

2 tablespoons (30 mL) dry sherry
4 teaspoons (20 mL) soy sauce
1 teaspoon (5 mL) vinegar
¼ teaspoon (1 mL) ground coriander seeds
¼ cup (50 mL) flour
¼ teaspoon (1 mL) pepper
1 pound (500 g) pork tenderloin, sliced thin
4 tablespoons (60 mL) vegetable oil, divided
1 medium onion, sliced thin
1 red bell pepper, sliced thin
2 tart apples, peeled, cored and sliced thin
1 garlic clove, crushed

In small bowl, combine sherry, soy sauce, vinegar and coriander; set aside.

Combine flour and pepper in plastic bag; add pork and shake to coat.

In large frypan or wok, heat two tablespoons (30 mL) oil. Shake excess flour off pork. Add pork to wok and cook over high heat for about two minutes or until well browned. With slotted spoon, remove pork to plate.

Add remaining two tablespoons (30 mL) oil to wok. Add onion and stir-fry over medium-high heat for two minutes. Add red pepper, apples and garlic; stir-fry for an additional two minutes. Return pork to wok. Add sherry mixture and stir until well mixed and heated through. ★

WHAT'S CORIANDER?

When it's a young green plant, we call it cilantro, and use the chopped leaves in any number of Mexican, East Indian, Chinese and Middle Eastern dishes.

Coriander, the adult plant, is a completely different culinary experience. "A combination of lemon, sage and caraway," says one authority, while another speaks of a "warm, sweet and orange-like aroma."

Buy whole coriander seeds and grind them as you need them, giving them a light roasting in a dry frying pan just before using them. Don't bother buying ground coriander: the ground spice quickly loses its flavor and aroma.

Lamb and Asparagus Stir-Fry

Makes four servings

You don't very often find a recipe for stir-fried lamb. For a special feature on stir-frying, we followed our own advice and applied the technique to lamb shoulder steaks to develop this recipe. Set the lamb to marinate for two hours in a mixture of sherry, soy sauce, ginger and five-spice powder, then stir-fry with asparagus – or green beans, if they're in season.

1½ pounds (750 g) lamb shoulder steaks, boned
1 egg white
2 garlic cloves, crushed
2 tablespoons (30 mL) dry sherry
1 tablespoon (15 mL) soy sauce
2 teaspoons (10 mL) finely chopped fresh ginger
¼ teaspoon (1 mL) five-spice powder
2 tablespoons (30 mL) vegetable oil, divided
1 pound (500 g) asparagus, cut diagonally into 1-inch (2.5-cm) pieces
5 green onions, cut diagonally into 2-inch (5-cm) pieces

Trim fat from lamb. Cut lamb into thin strips; set aside.

In small bowl, stir together egg white, garlic, sherry, soy sauce, ginger and five-spice powder. Stir in lamb strips. Cover and refrigerate for about two hours.

In wok, heat one tablespoon (15 mL) oil over high heat. Add lamb mixture and stir-fry for three to five minutes or until meat changes color. With slotted spoon, remove lamb to plate. Add remaining one tablespoon (15 mL) oil to wok and heat. Add asparagus and green onions and stir-fry for two minutes or until asparagus is tender-crisp. Return meat and heat through. ★

Beef Stir-Fry with Mangoes and Fresh Ginger

Makes four servings

Of course, you could just eat your mangoes out of hand, and for the first ones of the season, there's no better way. But when you've had plenty of mangoes all by themselves, consider using them to turn a pound of flank steak into an exotic stir-fry. For even more color, make a snow pea and red pepper salad, the snow peas in bite-size pieces, the red pepper cut into match sticks. Dress it with a vinaigrette made from vinegar, a mild-tasting vegetable oil (olive oil is too assertive) and a dash of Chinese sesame oil.

1 (1-pound or 500-g) flank steak, sliced thin
2 tablespoons (30 mL) soy sauce
1 teaspoon (5 mL) finely chopped fresh ginger
1 garlic clove, chopped fine
Pinch dried crushed hot red pepper
2 tablespoons (30 mL) vegetable oil
2 mangoes, peeled and sliced
2 green onions, chopped

Sauce:

¼ cup (50 mL) beef stock
1 tablespoon (15 mL) soy sauce
2 teaspoons (10 mL) cornstarch
¼ teaspoon (1 mL) salt

Place beef strips in large bowl. Combine two tablespoons (30 mL) soy sauce, ginger, garlic and hot pepper; pour over meat and toss to coat.

In separate bowl, combine sauce ingredients; set aside.

Heat wok or large frypan over high heat for about one minute. Add oil and heat. Add beef and stir-fry until browned, about three minutes. Add sauce mixture and bring to a boil. Add mangoes and green onions and heat through. ★

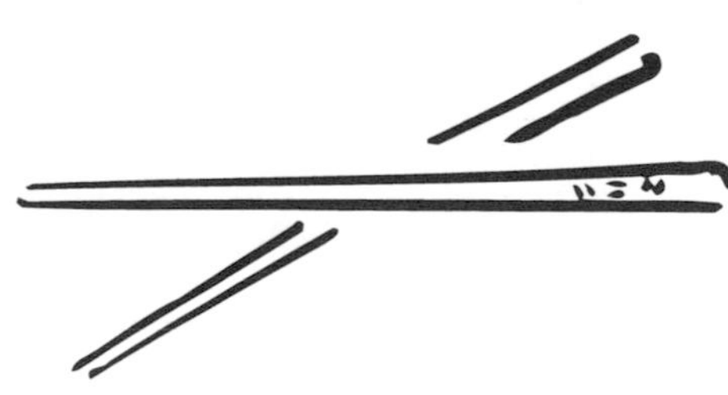

MANAGING MANGOES

A mango is ripe when its flesh yields to gentle pressure and when you get intoxicated sniffing the stem end.

Don't try to gauge ripeness by color. A Tommy Atkins mango doesn't turn yellow as it ripens, and ripe fruit can still show some green. A Haden is ripe when it turns yellow.

It's okay to buy mangoes green. Let your mangoes ripen at room temperature; when they're ripe, eat them. Don't put a mango in the fridge for more than an hour, just before eating. Mangoes stored in the fridge for a day or two will lose flavor and they may blacken around the stem.

Putting the Rim on the Grill

The May 24th weekend officially marks the beginning of the barbecue season here, but there are always people jumping the gun. No wonder: grilling gives us food touched by fire, easy, outdoorsy and uncomplicated.

You'll find other five-star barbecue recipes scattered throughout the book. This section brings together thrills from the grill with a decidedly Pacific Rim flavor.

Halibut in Fiery Ginger Sauce

Makes four servings

We used fresh halibut when we tested this recipe and are inclined, come to think of it, to find ways to use fresh halibut whenever we can get it. Cod, snapper or swordfish would work just fine too.

3 tablespoons (45 mL) chopped fresh ginger
2 garlic cloves, chopped fine
2 tablespoons (30 mL) sesame seeds
2 tablespoons (30 mL) sesame oil
2 tablespoons (30 mL) soy sauce
2 teaspoons (10 mL) anchovy paste
1 teaspoon (5 mL) sugar
½ teaspoon (2 mL) Tabasco sauce
1 cup (250 mL) water
2 teaspoons (10 mL) cornstarch
½ cup (125 mL) sliced green onions
4 halibut steaks, about 1-inch (2.5-cm) thick
Vegetable oil

In medium saucepan, saute ginger, garlic and sesame seeds in hot sesame oil for one minute. Stir in soy sauce, anchovy paste, sugar and Tabasco sauce; cook two minutes, stirring constantly.

Combine water and cornstarch. Stir into saucepan and cook until mixture boils and thickens, stirring constantly. Boil one minute. Stir in green onions.

Brush halibut lightly with vegetable oil. Place in well greased hinged wire rack holder. Place on barbecue over high heat for five to seven minutes per side, brushing occasionally with additional oil.

Spoon some of the warm sauce over each halibut steak. Serve remaining sauce separately. ★

Almost Chicken Tikka

Makes six servings

Chicken tikka is one of the most appealing of all East Indian dishes: boneless chicken breasts marinated in yogurt and spices and then seared in the inferno of all-around heat that's known as a tandoori oven. You can't do that on a barbecue, which is why our recipe, given to us by Amin Jamal of the Rubina Tandoori restaurant, is called Almost Chicken Tikka. Delicious and easy, it requires only the most minimal of last-minute attention.

4 whole chicken breasts, boned and skinned
1 cup (250 mL) 2 per cent plain yogurt
10 garlic cloves, peeled
1 (3-inch or 7-cm) piece fresh ginger, peeled and cut into ½-inch (1-cm) pieces
2 teaspoons (10 mL) ground cumin
1 fresh hot red or green chili pepper, halved and seeded
2 teaspoons (10 mL) salt
Generous pinch saffron, softened in 1 teaspoon (5 mL) hot water
6 drops yellow food coloring, about (optional)
3 drops red food coloring, about (optional)

Trim any excess fat from chicken. Cut chicken into about 1½-inch (4-cm) chunks and place in large bowl.

In food processor, combine yogurt, garlic, ginger, cumin, chili pepper, salt and saffron. Mix together yellow and red food coloring to make an orange color. Add to yogurt mixture and process until smooth. Pour over chicken and let marinate in refrigerator for 24 hours.

Remove chicken pieces from marinade and thread on to skewers. Place on barbecue grill and cook until done, turning once. ★

Indonesian Chicken Sate with Rice

Makes six servings

Boneless strips of chicken give you grilled chicken without the horror of meat cooked black on the outside, red on the inside. The secret to this recipe is the cup of toasted almonds, pureed in the blender, mixed into a marinade and left to work their magic in the fridge overnight. If you need a recipe today, you can marinate the chicken for only two hours with good results, but in that case you miss out on the thrill of making a company dinner in less than half an hour.

- **1 cup (250 mL) toasted almonds**
- **¼ cup (50 mL) soy sauce**
- **1 (284-mL) can chicken broth, divided**
- **6 tablespoons (90 mL) vegetable oil, divided**
- **2 tablespoons (30 mL) lemon juice**
- **2 tablespoons (30 mL) sugar**
- **2 garlic cloves, chopped fine**
- **¾ teaspoon (4 mL) ground ginger**
- **¼ teaspoon (1 mL) cayenne pepper**
- **3 large whole chicken breasts, boned, skinned and halved**
- **1½ cups (375 mL) chopped onions**
- **1½ cups (375 mL) long-grain rice**
- **¼ cup (50 mL) chopped parsley**

Place almonds in blender or food processor and process until finely chopped.

In large bowl, combine almonds, soy sauce, ¼ cup (50 mL) chicken broth, two tablespoons (30 mL) oil, lemon juice, sugar, garlic, ginger and cayenne pepper; set aside.

Cut each chicken breast into three strips. Add chicken strips to almond mixture and place in refrigerator for at least two hours, or overnight.

In 10-inch (25.5-cm) frypan, heat remaining four tablespoons (60 mL) oil. Add onions and rice; cook for five minutes, stirring constantly. Add water to remaining chicken broth to measure three cups (750 mL); stir into rice. Simmer, covered, for 20 minutes. Stir in parsley.

Skewer chicken strips lengthwise on to skewers. Brush chicken with almond marinade. Grill or broil chicken, about 3 inches (7 cm) from heat, for about seven minutes per side, brushing occasionally with marinade. Serve on bed of rice. ★

Beef Strips with Hoisin and Sherry

Makes six servings

Hoisin sauce, a chocolate-colored mix of soybeans, garlic, chili peppers and spices, is one of the most instantly appealing condiments in the Chinese cupboard.

Make time your ally by slicing the flank steak and setting it to marinate overnight. When you're ready to cook the steak, thread it on to skewers. The beef will be remarkably tender.

1 flank steak, about 1½ pounds (750 g)

Marinade:

¼ cup (50 mL) Hoisin sauce
¼ cup (50 mL) dry sherry
2 tablespoons (30 mL) soy sauce
1 tablespoon (15 mL) sesame oil
4 green onions, sliced
1 teaspoon (5 mL) grated fresh ginger

Cut flank steak across the grain into ¼-inch (5-mm) thick slices; place in small bowl.

Combine marinade ingredients and pour over meat strips, stirring to coat meat well. Cover and marinate in refrigerator at least four hours, preferably overnight.

Remove beef strips from marinade; reserve marinade. Thread beef strips lengthwise on to skewers in an interlacing fashion. Place on barbecue grill and cook three to four minutes per side, basting with remaining marinade. ★

HOISIN SAUCE

Most people meet hoisin sauce for the first time when eating Peking duck, for which reason it's sometimes also called Peking sauce.

Instantly appealing, this mixture of soybeans, garlic, chili peppers and various spices can find its way into a lot of dishes if you let it.

Try grilling split Japanese eggplants, cut-side down, then flipping them over and basting the grilled side with hoisin.

Or spread a little hoisin inside a flour tortilla and add finely chopped stir-fried vegetables for light cross-cultural lunch.

If you buy hoisin sauce in a can, move the contents to a non-metal container once it's opened. All opened containers of hoisin sauce should be stored in the fridge.

Beef Sate with Spicy Szechuan Sauce

Makes 24 skewers

Most of the time we think of grilling as a summer occupation. This recipe for beef sate could, of course, be cooked on a hibachi on the back deck. But we used it as part of a December story on finger food with substance for holiday parties. If you're planning to use the barbecue, thread the beef pieces on to larger skewers.

- ¾ **pound (350 g) beef filet, cut into 24 (3x1-inch or 7x2.5-cm) thin strips**

Marinade:

- ½ **cup (125 mL) soy sauce**
- 1 **tablespoon (15 mL) liquid honey**
- 1 **teaspoon (5 mL) dried crushed hot red pepper**
- ½ **teaspoon (2 mL) ground cumin**
- ½ **teaspoon (2 mL) turmeric**

Szechuan Sauce:

- 3 **tablespoons (45 mL) unsalted butter, divided**
- 1 **garlic clove, chopped fine**
- 1 **small green onion, chopped fine**
- ½ **cup (125 mL) chicken stock**
- 2 **tablespoons (30 mL) soy sauce**
- ½ **teaspoon (2 mL) dried crushed hot red pepper**

Using 24 (6-inch or 15-cm) bamboo skewers, stick a skewer into each strip of meat lengthwise and arrange in large baking dish. Refrigerate until needed.

For marinade: In small bowl, combine all the marinade ingredients and pour over meat, turning to coat all sides. Let marinate about 15 minutes.

Preheat broiler while the steak is marinating.

For sauce: In small frypan, melt one tablespoon (15 mL) butter. Add garlic and green onion; saute over medium-high heat until soft, about two minutes. Add stock, soy sauce and hot red pepper; cook an additional one or two minutes. Strain into a clean small saucepan; whisk in remaining two tablespoons (30 mL) butter. Keep warm.

Arrange skewers of meat on broiler pan and place under broiler about 4 to 5 inches (10 to 12.5 cm) from heat. Broil for two

WHERE'S THE BEEF?

When a recipe calls for thin slices of beef, the meat ought to be in the freezer. Put it there, wrapped in plastic, an hour before you plan to start slicing.

The partially frozen meat is firmer than meat at room temperature. That firmness helps keep your slices neat and regular.

Cut across the grain for the most tender meat.

minutes, turn skewers over and broil another one minute or until medium-rare.

Pour sauce into small bowl and set in centre of large serving platter. Arrange skewers around bowl and serve immediately. ★

Spicy Grilled Pork Chops with Oranges and Cumin

Makes four servings

These chops marinate overnight, stuffed with onions, garlic, chili powder, cumin and oranges. By the time you pull them out of the fridge to barbecue them, they're imbued with tropical flavor.

- **¼ cup (50 mL) vegetable oil**
- **¼ cup (50 mL) finely chopped onions**
- **2 garlic cloves, chopped fine**
- **4 teaspoons (20 mL) chili powder**
- **½ teaspoon (2 mL) ground cumin**
- **¼ teaspoon (1 mL) salt**
- **4 oranges, divided**
- **4 loin pork chops, about 1½-inches (4-cm) thick**

In small saucepan, combine oil, onions, garlic, chili powder, cumin and salt. Grate one tablespoon (15 mL) rind from one orange; add to mixture in saucepan. Cook over medium heat for four to five minutes, stirring constantly. Squeeze juice from two oranges and add to mixture in saucepan; set marinade aside.

Peel remaining two oranges and section; set aside.

With a sharp knife, cut a pocket in each pork chop. Spoon some of the marinade and an equal portion of orange sections in each pocket. Place pork chops in shallow pan or plastic bag with remaining marinade. Marinate in refrigerator for six hours or overnight, turning occasionally.

Remove chops from marinade; reserve marinade. Place chops on barbecue grill over high heat; brown chops on both sides. Reduce heat to low and cook chops for 30 to 40 minutes or until cooked, brushing frequently with marinade and turning occasionally. ★

★ ★ ★ ★ ★

A Duet of Noodle Recipes

Stephen Wong, our Pacific Rim columnist, brought us two noodle recipes to accompany his first story marking Chinese New Year. The connection? Noodles have an age-old association with long life. By eating long strands of noodles, breakfast, lunch and dinner, you can ensure that some of that longevity will rub off on you – rather like the tradition that each different Christmas cake you sample guarantees one happy month in the new year.

Don't let the list of ingredients put you off. Once everything's assembled, these recipes are quick and easy.

Singapore Stir-Fried Rice Noodles

Makes four to six servings

Singapore noodles can be a one-dish meal, or, if you have more people to feed, a main dish accompanied by stir-fried greens.

Rice vermicelli, also called rice-stick noodle, is popular in Southeast Asia. It requires only soaking in cold water before it's added to the other ingredients. The yellow chives called for in the recipe have a mild onion flavor. Grown without exposure to sunlight, they do not turn green. If you aren't able to find them, use regular green chives.

8½ ounces (250 g) rice vermicelli (not cellophane noodles)
1½ teaspoons (7 mL) cornstarch
Pinch salt
2 eggs, divided
6 ounces (170 g) shelled small raw shrimp
6 tablespoons (90 mL) vegetable oil, divided
6 ounces (170 g) barbecued pork, cut into thin strips
½ cup (125 mL) diagonally sliced celery (about 1-inch or 2.5-cm pieces)
1 cup (250 mL) tightly packed bean sprouts
1 teaspoon (4 mL) salt, divided
½ cup (125 mL) sliced yellow chives (about 1-inch or 2.5-cm pieces)
1 tablespoon (15 mL) curry powder
1 cup (250 mL) chicken stock
1 tablespoon (15 mL) light soy sauce
¼ teaspoon (1 mL) sugar
¼ teaspoon (1 mL) pepper

SOY SAUCE SUBTLETIES

Soy sauce is made by fermenting mashed soybeans and roasted grains such as wheat, barley or rice. Salt is then added and the mixture is filtered after a period of aging.

That said, there are as many variations on soy sauce as there are Asian nations.

In general: light soy sauce is thinner and saltier than dark. It is used to impart a depth of flavor to ingredients without masking their essential tastes and colors.

Dark soy sauce has a richer aroma than light soy and a sweeter taste, because of added sugar or molasses. It is used when a deep color is needed in a dish.

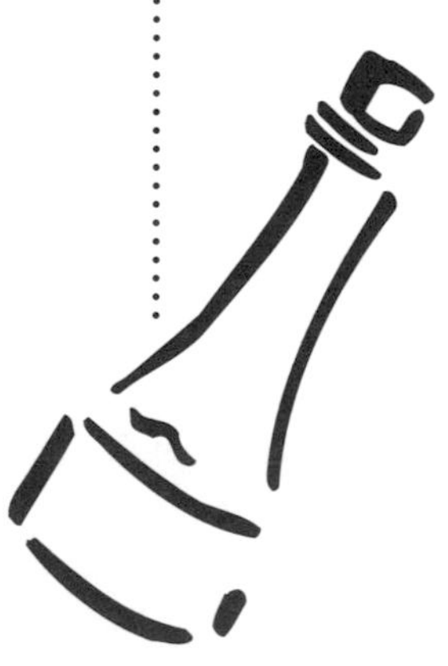

Soak noodles in cold water until soft, about 15 minutes; drain and set aside.

In small bowl, combine cornstarch, pinch salt and one tablespoon (15 mL) of egg white. Stir in shrimp; let stand for five minutes.

In separate bowl, lightly beat remainder of eggs. In wok, heat one tablespoon (15 mL) oil. Pour in eggs and swirl to form a thin layer on bottom of pan. When cooked, remove from wok and cut into 1-inch (2.5-cm) strips; set aside.

Add two tablespoons (30 mL) oil to wok and heat. Add shrimp, pork, celery and bean sprouts; stir-fry for two minutes. Season with ½ teaspoon (2 mL) salt. Stir in yellow chives and cooked eggs; immediately remove mixture from wok and set aside.

Heat remaining three tablespoons (45 mL) oil in wok over medium-high heat. Add curry powder and stir for 10 seconds. Add noodles and toss well. Add chicken stock, soy sauce, sugar, remaining ½ teaspoon (2 mL) salt and pepper; mix well. Cover and cook over low heat for three minutes. Stir in shrimp mixture. Cook over medium-high heat until sauce is absorbed. Place on platter or in individual bowls and serve immediately. ★

Peppered Beef with Shanghai Noodles

Makes four servings

Shanghai noodles are wheat noodles, first made in Northern China. With their help, you get a luxurious one-dish meal that stretches half a pound of sirloin into dinner for four. You can buy Shanghai noodles cooked and wrapped in plastic in Chinatown stores.

- **½ pound (250 g) sirloin steak**
- **4 tablespoons (60 mL) vegetable oil, divided**
- **1 small shallot, chopped fine**
- **1 garlic clove, chopped fine**
- **¾ teaspoon (4 mL) freshly ground pepper or to taste**
- **½ cup (125 mL) green bell pepper strips (1-inch or 2.5-cm long)**
- **½ cup (125 mL) red bell pepper strips (1-inch or 2.5-cm long)**
- **1 cup (250 mL) tightly packed bean sprouts**
- **1½ pounds (750 g) cooked Shanghai noodles**

Marinade:

- **1 tablespoon (15 mL) oyster sauce**
- **1½ teaspoons (7 mL) dark soy sauce**
- **1½ teaspoons (7 mL) cornstarch**
- **¼ teaspoon (1 mL) sugar**
- **½ teaspoon (2 mL) salt**

Sauce:

- **1 teaspoon (5 mL) light soy sauce**
- **1 tablespoon (15 mL) dark soy sauce**
- **½ teaspoon (2 mL) sugar**

Cut beef into thin strips.

Combine marinade ingredients in bowl. Add beef and marinate for 20 minutes.

Heat wok and add two tablespoons (30 mL) oil. Add shallot, garlic and ground pepper; stir for 10 seconds. Add beef with marinade and stir for one minute. Add bell peppers and bean sprouts; stir for an additional two minutes and set aside.

Heat remaining two tablespoons (30 mL) oil over medium heat. Add noodles and stir constantly for one minute. Add sauce ingredients and cook for two minutes, stirring constantly. Add beef and bell pepper mixture; mix well. Stir-fry until heated through. Season to taste with more pepper if desired. Serve immediately. ★

★ ★ ★ ★ ★

Tropical Sweets

It's a marvel, living in a place where boxes of mangoes are something to buy in the supermarket and take home, like boxes of apples. Until you get over the surprise of mangoes, it seems like anything more complicated than just carving them up and eating them is too much trouble. But sooner or later you want something fancier. The same goes for papayas and persimmons. Here are three suggestions, more dramatic than fresh fruit, less complicated than you'd think possible.

Mango Ice Cream

Makes about one quart (1 L)

You can't buy an ice cream with a more intense mango flavor than this one. Make it for a dramatic but ridiculously easy end to a summer dinner party. If you must have excess, serve a tray of bittersweet chocolate hearts with the ice cream.

- **1 cup (250 mL) milk, divided**
- **¼ cup (50 mL) plus 3 tablespoons (45 mL) sugar**
- **⅛ teaspoon (0.5 mL) salt**
- **1 cup (250 mL) whipping cream**
- **1½ cups (375 mL) mango puree (about 2 large mangoes)**
- **1½ teaspoons (7 mL) vanilla**

In small saucepan, heat ½ cup (125 mL) milk until just lukewarm. Add sugar and salt; stir until sugar is dissolved. Stir in remaining ½ cup (125 mL) milk. Pour into bowl; cover and chill thoroughly in refrigerator, about three hours.

Add cream, mango puree and vanilla to milk mixture. Pour into ice cream maker and freeze according to manufacturer's directions. ★

ICE DREAM

If a cup of whipping cream seems to you to be an unconscionable amount of fat to add to a dessert, you can, of course, make Mango Ice Cream with light cream, or even whole milk.

But let's have no delusions: the lower the fat content, the less voluptuous the ice cream. If you go so far as to use skim milk, you'll have a grainy mango slush on your hands. That's not necessarily a bad thing to have, but it's also not the knockout punch of fruit and cream that so delighted us when we made it.

Tropical Pancake

Makes two servings

Dessert for four or brunch for two, this is an endlessly mutable, very easy, oven-baked pancake. Papaya is my favorite fruit filling, although mangoes are nice too. For the sauce, I like blackberries best, but raspberries are almost as good and more readily available. Or, if the opportunity arises, you might scoop out the pulp and seeds of a ripe passion fruit for the most instant of sauces.

1½ tablespoons (22 mL) unsalted butter
3 large eggs, beaten
¾ cup (175 mL) milk
½ teaspoon (2 mL) salt
¾ cup (175 mL) all-purpose flour
1 cup (250 mL) frozen unsweetened raspberries, thawed
1 tablespoon (15 mL) liquid honey, about
2 teaspoons (10 mL) orange-flavored liqueur, optional
1 papaya, peeled and sliced thin
Sifted icing sugar

In 12-inch (30.5-cm) cast iron frypan, melt butter.

Combine beaten eggs, milk and salt in bowl; beat well. Add flour and beat until batter is smooth; pour into frypan.

Bake at 450 F (230 C) for 10 minutes, pricking batter with a fork or skewer when it puffs up in large bubbles. Reduce heat to 350 F (180 C) and bake an additional five minutes, pricking if necessary.

While pancake is baking, puree raspberries and sieve to remove seeds. Sweeten to taste with honey and add orange-flavored liqueur.

When pancake is baked, arrange papaya slices over half of pancake. Drizzle with some raspberry puree. Fold other half of pancake over papaya slices. Slide on to serving plate and dust with icing sugar. (Extra puree can be served alongside or refrigerated for serving over ice cream.) ★

Broiled Persimmon Halves with Brown Sugar

Makes two servings

Fuyu persimmons are little orange globes that looked like flattened baseballs. But for sheer sensuality, I prefer Hachiya persimmons – the ones with a point at one end and a four-petalled stem, like a green flower, at the other.

Eating an unripe Hachiya is an unforgettably puckery experience. To avoid this, wait until the fruit looks seriously overripe, and the flesh under the slightly wrinkled skin feels softer than a baby's cheeks.

When you've had enough persimmons au naturel, try topping them with a sprinkling of brown sugar and sliding them under the broiler for a minute for the speediest of exotic desserts.

1 ripe Hachiya persimmon
3 teaspoons (14 mL) brown sugar, divided
1½ teaspoons (8 mL) cold butter, divided
Dairy sour cream, optional

Cut out leaf end of persimmon, then halve fruit lengthwise. With a sharp knife, cut around fruit, close to the skin, to free the flesh. Do not remove from skin.

Sprinkle 1½ teaspoons (7 mL) brown sugar evenly over each half; dot each side with ¾ teaspoon (4 mL) butter.

Broil 3 inches (7 cm) from heat for about one minute or until sugar bubbles. Serve with sour cream. ★

Ciao Italian Style

The Antipasto Meal

★

Pizza and Other Breads with Pizazz

★

Pasta for any Occasion

★

Three Ways to Cook Chicken Pronto

★

Two Easy Ways with Fish Fillets

No kitchen is an island. We swim in the world of food, and right now, the strongest current is Italian. Food analysts say that in every European country, Italian food ranks second in popularity after the national cuisine. You can't avoid pizza in North America; you can even eat pizza in Bali if you want to – a competently made pizza, cooked in a brick oven over a coffee-wood fire.

The reasons are obvious enough. Modern Italian food offers simple, direct flavors and easy preparation, made easier still when there's a good Italian deli nearby, offering fresh pasta, marinated vegetables, sun-dried tomatoes and bocconcini.

In the test kitchen, we often reach for basil and olive oil, garlic and parmesan. And why not? We like the results and so do our taste panels.

★ ★ ★ ★ ★

THE ANTIPASTO MEAL

In the summer I love to make antipasto platters: marinated artichoke hearts and vegetables, plenty of olives, an Italian tuna and potato salad, lightly cooked green beans generously flecked with fresh herbs, raw fennel, for its clean crunch, cheese, and, for the carnivores, prosciutto.

I know this is not the sort of dinner Italians eat, but, sometimes, breaking gastronomic rules is the only sensible thing to do. As long as you have wine, bread and the sort of friends who like to eat family style, from one big platter, you're golden. Four of the next five recipes started life as vegetable side dishes, and the serving sizes reflect that. They're also food I'd choose for an antipasto platter.

Herbed Green Beans

Makes four servings

This is the best way I know to cook green beans: shiny with olive oil, garlicky, salty, and generously covered in fresh herbs. They are irresistible hot from the pan, even better at room temperature and still seductive cold, the next day.

1 pound (500 g) green beans, trimmed
2 tablespoons (30 mL) olive oil
1 garlic clove, crushed
¼ teaspoon (1 mL) salt
1 tablespoon (15 mL) chopped fresh basil

Steam beans for four to five minutes or until tender-crisp.

When beans are almost cooked, heat oil and garlic over medium heat in large frypan. Add salt to frypan; remove beans from steamer and immediately add to frypan. Stir to coat with oil.

Transfer beans to bowl and sprinkle with basil; toss. Serve at room temperature. ★

KITCHEN DRAMA

When you make these beans, be sure to plan your cooking time so you can move them quickly from the steamer to the frypan.

As soon as they've reached the critical point – still crisp, but hot through, deep green and beaded with water droplets – salt the frypan and drop the beans, screaming hot, into the garlic-flavored oil.

Use whatever fresh herbs you have on hand. Basil is wonderful. Young, mild, fresh tarragon tastes good too, as do oregano and marjoram, on their own, or mixed with parsley or cilantro.

Roasted Bell Peppers in Balsamic Vinegar

Makes six servings

Whenever I see handsome red peppers at a decent price, I buy lots, roast them and marinate them. They keep all week, covered, in the fridge.

4 large red bell peppers
2 tablespoons (30 mL) thinly sliced fresh basil
2 tablespoons (30 mL) balsamic or cider vinegar

¼ **cup (50 mL) olive oil**
Salt to taste

Broil peppers on a baking sheet, turning several times until the skin is charred, about 20 to 30 minutes. Drop the peppers into a brown paper bag, roll the top shut, and let them sit until they are cool enough to handle.

Peel peppers, remove core and seeds. Cut in long wide strips and place in serving bowl. Add basil.

Place vinegar in small bowl. Gradually whisk in oil. Season with salt. Pour over peppers and basil and marinate in the refrigerator for several hours or overnight. ★

Asparagus with Pine Nuts and Fresh Herbs

Makes four to five servings

Almost any vegetable can star on an antipasto plate – but some, like asparagus, are more dramatic than others. Cook your asparagus gently and top it with toasted pine nuts, a lemon dressing and fresh basil and oregano.

1¼ **pounds (625 g) asparagus**
2 **tablespoons (30 mL) pine nuts**
¼ **cup (50 mL) olive oil**
1 **tablespoon (15 mL) fresh lemon juice**
1 **garlic clove, chopped fine**
¼ **teaspoon (1 mL) sugar**
2 **teaspoons (10 mL) finely chopped fresh oregano**
2 **teaspoons (10 mL) finely chopped fresh basil**
Salt and freshly ground pepper to taste

Snap off tough ends of asparagus. Cook in small amount of boiling water until tender-crisp. Drain and plunge immediately into ice water for a few minutes. Drain well and cut into 2-inch (5-cm) lengths. Set aside.

In small heavy frypan, toast pine nuts until evenly browned, shaking pan frequently. Remove from pan and cool.

Whisk together olive oil, lemon juice, garlic, sugar, oregano, basil, salt and pepper and pour over cool asparagus. Let stand about 30 minutes. Sprinkle with nuts. ★

Grilled Pepper Sunburst with Olives and Feta Cheese

Makes six to eight servings

If you'd like to make a production out of peppers, try this recipe. The peppers are flavored with a garlicky mixture of olive oil and balsamic vinegar, then grilled, sliced and laid out in whatever color arrangement suits your fancy. A final touch: a scattering of feta cheese, chopped fresh herbs and kalamata olives.

Balsamic Basting Sauce:

- **3 garlic cloves**
- **1 teaspoon (5 mL) salt**
- **3 tablespoons (45 mL) balsamic vinegar**
- **¼ cup (50 mL) olive oil**
- **½ teaspoon (2 mL) freshly ground pepper**

Other Ingredients:

- **2 pounds (1 kg) bell peppers (red, yellow and orange)**
- **Salt and freshly ground pepper to taste**
- **2 teaspoons (10 mL) finely chopped fresh oregano**
- **1 teaspoon (5 mL) finely chopped fresh thyme**
- **1 teaspoon (5 mL) finely chopped fresh rosemary**
- **¼ pound (125 g) feta cheese, drained and cut into ½-inch (1-cm) cubes**
- **12 to 16 kalamata olives**
- **1 tablespoon (15 mL) balsamic vinegar**

For basting sauce: Mash garlic and salt to a paste in a mortar with a pestle (see note). Place in small bowl. Whisk in balsamic vinegar, olive oil and pepper; set aside.

Core, seed and cut bell peppers into thirds. Brush both sides of peppers with sauce and place in large bowl. Pour remaining sauce over top.

Remove peppers from sauce; reserving sauce. Place peppers skin-side down on greased barbecue rack over medium-high heat for six to eight minutes or until lightly charred but not mushy, basting with sauce and turning every three minutes. Slice peppers

THE COLOR OF PEPPERS

No wonder we like sweet red bell peppers so much: they're really just green peppers that have had an extra two to three weeks to get sweetly ripe on the vine.

Yellow and orange bell peppers start out green too and change color as they ripen.

Only purple bell peppers – which are green inside – begin life with a purple skin and stay that way. But purple peppers fade to khaki when heated: don't pay premium prices for the purple color if you plan to cook them.

into ½-inch (1-cm) wide strips. Arrange on a platter, alternating colors. Season with salt and pepper. Sprinkle with fresh herbs, feta and olives. Drizzle the one tablespoon (15 mL) balsamic vinegar over peppers.

Note: If you don't have a mortar and pestle, garlic can be mashed on a board using a fork. ★

Potato and Tuna Salad with Capers and Dijon Dressing

Makes two or three servings

This recipe is one of those simple little kitchen treasures: a salad capable of sustaining life, made from food you normally keep on hand. It gives heft to antipasto plate suppers, and makes a nice lunch the next day with – should you be so lucky – the leftover green beans.

- **2 medium potatoes**
- **2 green onions, sliced**
- **1 (184-g) can tuna, drained**
- **3 tablespoons (45 mL) white wine vinegar**
- **3 tablespoons (45 mL) virgin olive oil**
- **1½ tablespoons (22 mL) finely chopped fresh parsley or cilantro**
- **2 tablespoons (30 mL) drained capers**
- **1 teaspoon (5 mL) Dijon mustard**
- **Salt and freshly ground pepper to taste**

Cook unpeeled potatoes in boiling water until tender. Drain and cool.

Peel and cube potatoes. Combine potatoes, green onions and tuna in bowl. In separate bowl, whisk together vinegar, olive oil, parsley, capers, mustard and salt and pepper. Pour over potato mixture and toss to coat. Serve at room temperature. ★

WHAT ARE CAPERS?

True capers are the unopened flower bud of the caper bush, which grows wild all around the Mediterranean. Capers are sold pickled in strongly salted wine vinegar. Good capers are olive green and firm to the touch; the smaller the caper, the better the flavor.

False capers are unripe nasturtium seeds, which, when pickled in salted vinegar, taste similar to capers.

Once you've opened a jar of capers, keep it in the fridge, and make sure there's enough liquid in the bottle to cover the capers. When capers are exposed to air, their taste turns nasty.

PIZZA AND OTHER BREADS WITH PIZAZZ

You can, of course, pick up a good loaf of bread, Italian or otherwise to eat with your antipasto. But if you have the time to make your own – and some of these breads are remarkably speedy – you'll be amply rewarded.

Feel free to play around: the quick pizza dough, for example, makes a fine pizza, but you can also use it as a springboard for a multitude of easy breads. My favorite deviation is to saute an onion in a little oil very gently while the dough rises, then spread the sauteed onion over the dough and sprinkle it with black, onion-fragrant kalonji seeds (often used in Bengali cooking and available at spice stores and ethnic markets) before I put it in the oven. The double onion flavor is wonderfully rich.

Quick Pizza Dough

Makes eight (6-inch or 15-cm) pizzas

This bread, adapted from a recipe in Eating Well magazine, has been part of my kitchen ever since we tested it. If you let the food processor do the kneading, it's unbelievably fast.

4 to 4½ cups (1 to 1.125 L) all-purpose flour
2 (8-g) packages instant yeast
2 teaspoons (10 mL) salt
1 teaspoon (5 mL) sugar
Water
2 teaspoons (10 mL) olive oil
Cornmeal

Food processor method: In large-capacity food processor fitted with a steel blade, combine four cups (1 L) flour, yeast, salt and sugar. Heat 1½ cups (375 mL) water and olive oil until very warm, 125 to 130 F (50 to 55 C). With the motor running, gradually pour the warm water mixture through the feed tube. Process, adding up to two tablespoons (30 mL) cold water until the dough forms a ball, then process for one minute to knead.

Turn dough out on to lightly floured surface, cover with plastic wrap and let rest for 10 minutes.

MORE DOUGH

This recipe makes enough pizza dough to serve four. If there are only two of you, make the whole recipe, let the dough rest 10 minutes after kneading, then punch it down and cut it in two. Put half into a plastic bag and refrigerate it.

The dough will keep 24 hours in the fridge. An hour before you want supper, take the dough out of its plastic bag and let it come to room temperature before baking.

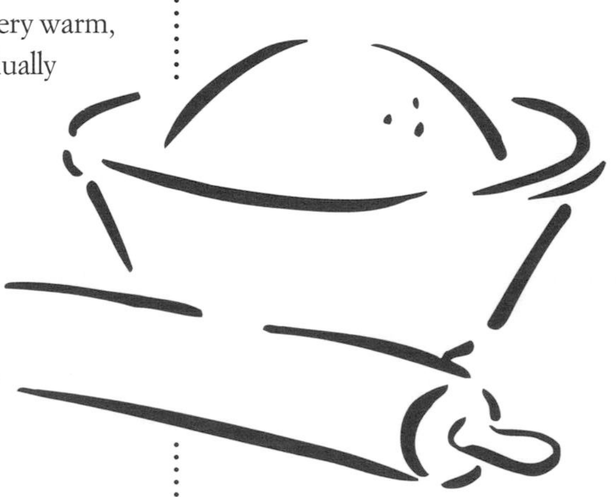

Conventional method: In large bowl, combine three cups (750 mL) of flour, yeast, salt and sugar. Heat 1¾ cups (425 mL) water and olive oil until very warm, 125 to 130 F (50 to 55 C). With wooden spoon, gradually stir the warm water mixture into flour mixture; beat until well mixed. Gradually add enough of the remaining flour to make a soft, but not sticky, dough.

Turn dough out on to a lightly floured surface and knead for eight to 10 minutes or until smooth and elastic, adding flour if needed. Cover with plastic wrap and let rest for 10 minutes.

To make pizza: Place an inverted large baking sheet on the lowest rack of the oven. Preheat oven to 500 F (260 C).

Divide pizza dough into eight pieces. Using your fists, stretch one piece into a 6-inch (15-cm) round. (Or roll out on a lightly floured surface with a rolling pin.) Keep remaining dough covered with a towel or plastic wrap as you work.

Place the round on a cornmeal-dusted inverted baking sheet. Stretch or roll a second round of dough and place beside the first. Top as desired.

Carefully slide the pizzas on to the hot baking sheet in oven. Bake for 10 to 14 minutes or until the bottoms are crisp and browned. Working with two pizzas at a time, repeat with the remaining dough. ★

Pizza Toppings

One day, musing idly on the question of pizza toppings, we decided to ask readers what they liked best. The letters we received showed a marked fondness for tomato sauce and mozzarella. But some of you went boldly where no pizza has gone before. We tested the recipes that looked best, and sat them out in front of a taste panel. Here are the five-star pizzas and their authors.

Barbecued Duck Pizza:

Brush pizza crust with hoisin sauce, top with small pieces of barbecued duck and sliced green onions. *(Duncan Lee, New Westminster)*

Black Bean Pizza:

Spread black bean sauce (recipe follows) on pizza crust. Sprinkle with grated monterey jack and cheddar cheese and top with drained, sliced black olives, diced red or green bell pepper and sliced green onions.

For black bean sauce: Place one (425-g) can black beans (rinsed and drained), three tablespoons (45 mL) olive oil, two tablespoons (30 mL) chopped fresh cilantro, one teaspoon (5 mL) cumin, one teaspoon (5 mL) Tabasco sauce and one finely chopped garlic clove in food processor and process until smooth. *(Richard Ketchen, West Vancouver)*

Salami, Sun-Dried Tomato and Oyster Mushroom Pizza:

Lightly brush pizza crust with pesto sauce, then spread with tomato sauce. Top with salami slices, sliced sun-dried tomatoes (packed in oil), chopped oyster mushrooms, freshly grated romano cheese and sliced oka cheese. *(Tina Perenseff, Vancouver)*

Spinach, Artichoke Heart and Mozzarella Pizza:

Spread tomato sauce on pizza crust. Cover with frozen chopped spinach (thawed and well-drained) and sprinkle with grated mozzarella combined with a little grated old cheddar cheese. Top with marinated artichoke hearts (cut in chunks), thickly sliced Sicilian olives and sliced sun-dried tomatoes (packed in oil). Arrange thinly sliced red onion rings over top; scatter with finely chopped jalapeno peppers and sprinkle with grated parmesan cheese. *(Denise Webb, Deep Bay, B.C.)*

Avocado and Pesto Pizza:

Spread pesto sauce on pizza crust. Top with frozen chopped spinach (thawed and well-drained), marinated artichoke hearts (cut in chunks), sliced avocado, a sprinkle of dried basil, thinly sliced mozzarella cheese and sliced sun-dried tomatoes (packed in oil); sprinkle with grated parmesan cheese. *(Robert Christy, West Vancouver)*

Yegads! Tofu Pizza:

Spread tomato sauce over pizza crust. Top with thinly sliced garlic, sliced sun-dried tomatoes (packed in oil), sliced mushrooms, roasted red pepper slices, feta cheese, bite-size pieces fresh spinach, mozzarella-flavored tofu slices (cut in triangular shapes) and grated mozzarella and parmesan cheese; sprinkle lightly with dried, crushed, hot red pepper. *(Chris Toda, Richmond)* ★

Fast Tomato Sauce with Fresh Herbs

Makes 1¼ cups (300 mL) sauce

When you want to prove you can indeed make a great pizza faster than anyone can bring it to your door, it helps to have a fast tomato sauce up your sleeve. Start by sauteing garlic and onions, skip the long step of cooking down tomatoes by opening a can of tomato sauce, and, at the last moment, crown your efforts with fresh herbs.

- 1 **tablespoon (15 mL) olive oil**
- 1 **medium onion, chopped fine**
- 2 **or 3 garlic cloves, sliced thin**
- 1 **(213-mL) can tomato sauce**
- 2 **tablespoons (30 mL) tomato paste**
- 1 **teaspoon (5 mL) sugar**
- **Salt and freshly ground pepper to taste**
- ¼ **cup (50 mL) chopped fresh parsley**
- 1 **tablespoon (15 mL) chopped fresh oregano**
- 1 **tablespoon (15 mL) chopped fresh basil**

In large heavy saucepan, heat oil over medium-high heat. Add onion and garlic and saute for three to five minutes or until onion is softened. Stir in tomato sauce, tomato paste, sugar, salt and pepper. Thin with a little water and simmer over low heat for 15 minutes, stirring occasionally. (Keep the consistency to that of ketchup, thinning with a little water if necessary.)

Just before spreading sauce over pizza, stir in parsley, oregano and basil. ★

DON'T WASTE TOMATO PASTE

Most recipes call for only a tablespoon or two of tomato paste, leaving you with the rest of the contents of the can. Put it in the fridge and sure enough you'll find it, weeks later, growing a fine crop of green mould.

The answer: clean out the tomato paste tin with a spatula, put the paste into a small freezer bag and freeze it.

You can, if you like, measure it first. I find it easier to just cut off the size I need from the frozen lump.

Grilled Pizza

Makes two pizzas

No, there will never be an end to the list of new things to cook on the barbecue. One innovation we're fond of is grilled pizza: bread as immediate as you can get it, a little charred around the edges, thin crusted and topped with intense, salty flavors. It all happens fast, so be sure to have the toppings ready before you put the dough on the grill.

Gas barbecues with dual controls work best for cooking pizza. Keep one side very hot for cooking the dough. Use the other side as an unheated work surface for flipping the dough once the first side is cooked and ready for topping.

Dough:

- ¼ **teaspoon (1 mL) sugar**
- ½ **cup (125 mL) lukewarm water**
- 1½ **teaspoons (7 mL) traditional active dry yeast**
- 1½ **tablespoons (22 mL) whole-wheat flour**
- ¾ **teaspoon (4 mL) salt**
- 1 **to 1¼ cups (250 to 300 mL) all-purpose flour**
- **Olive oil**

Prosciutto Topping:

- ¼ **cup (50 mL) tomato sauce**
- 3 **tablespoons (45 mL) grated fresh parmesan cheese**
- 2 **tablespoons (30 mL) grated mozzarella cheese**
- 1 **small red bell pepper, seeded and julienned**
- 5 **thin slices prosciutto ham, cut in thin strips (about 3-inches or 7-cm long)**

Pepper and Olive Topping:

- ¼ **cup (50 mL) tomato sauce**
- 1 **garlic clove, chopped fine**
- 2 **tablespoons (30 mL) grated fresh parmesan cheese**
- ½ **cup (125 mL) grated mozzarella cheese**
- 1 **jalapeno pepper, seeded and chopped fine (about 1 tablespoon or 15 mL)**
- 2 **tablespoons (30 mL) kalamata olives, pitted and quartered**

THE ISSUE OF VIRGINITY

The most important thing to know about olive oil is this: you can taste the difference that extra-virgin oil makes, as long as it's cold.

For drizzling over bruschetta, or lush ripe tomatoes, or tender salad greens just picked from your own garden, cold-pressed extra-virgin olive oil is worth every penny it costs.

If you're going to saute vegetables, fry fish or chicken, or add olive oil to a bread dough, use either virgin or pure. Heat drives off the more subtle flavors of expensive oils.

For dough: In large bowl, dissolve sugar in water. Sprinkle yeast over top and let stand in warm place for about 10 minutes or until foamy; stir.

Add whole-wheat flour and salt to yeast mixture; stir to combine.

Stir in enough all-purpose flour to form a soft dough.

Turn dough out on to floured surface and knead for about five minutes or until smooth and elastic, kneading in additional flour as necessary. Place in greased bowl, turning dough to grease top. Cover and let rise in warm place until double in size, about 45 minutes.

Punch dough down and cut in half. Roll each piece, on oiled sheet of foil, into a circle about 9 inches (23 cm) in diameter. Brush tops with oil.

Flip one piece of dough on to barbecue grill over high heat, peel off foil. Cook about one minute or until underside is cooked. With tongs or spatula, gently loosen dough and slide over to edge of grill away from the heat.

Flip dough over and quickly brush top surface with oil. Arrange prosciutto topping ingredients over cooked surface in the order listed. With spatula or tongs, slide pizza back over the heat and cook until underside is done and cheese is melted, about one to two minutes.

Repeat with remaining dough and pepper and olive topping ingredients. ★

Calzone with Ricotta and Pesto

Makes four servings

Calzone is a closed pizza, the dough wrapped around a filling which stays, by virtue of being inside the crust, much more meltingly soft than a topping. In this case, a rich-tasting yeast dough encloses a classic basil-and-pine-nut pesto, smoothed out by ricotta cheese. Rebecca Dawson, who wrote our vegetarian column for one year, contributed this recipe as part of a story on savory vegetarian pies.

Dough:

- **1 teaspoon (5 mL) sugar**
- **2 tablespoons (30 mL) lukewarm water**
- **1 (8-g) package traditional active dry yeast**
- **1 large egg**
- **3 tablespoons (45 mL) olive oil, divided**
- **½ cup (125 mL) lukewarm milk**
- **2 cups (500 mL) unbleached all-purpose flour**
- **1 teaspoon (5 mL) salt**

Pesto With Ricotta:

- **4 large garlic cloves, peeled**
- **1 cup (250 mL) basil leaves and stems**
- **¼ cup (50 mL) pine nuts**
- **½ cup (125 mL) olive oil**
- **½ cup (125 mL) grated parmesan cheese**
- **1 cup (250 mL) ricotta cheese**
- **Salt and freshly ground pepper to taste**

For dough: Dissolve sugar in lukewarm water. Sprinkle yeast over and let stand in warm place for 10 minutes or until dissolved; stir.

In separate bowl, mix together egg, one tablespoon (15 mL) olive oil and milk. Add yeast mixture and stir to combine.

In large bowl, combine flour and salt. Add milk mixture and mix to form a ball.

Turn dough out on to lightly floured surface and knead for seven to 10 minutes or until smooth and elastic, adding additional flour as needed.

Place dough in lightly oiled bowl, turning to grease top. Cover with plastic wrap and let rise in warm place until doubled in size, about 45 minutes.

While dough is rising make pesto. Place garlic and basil in food processor; pulse to coarsely chop. Add pine nuts and pulse. With machine running, pour in olive oil. Place pesto in bowl and stir in parmesan cheese. Gently stir in ricotta cheese. Season to taste with salt and pepper.

Punch dough down and divide into four equal pieces; cover and let rest for 15 minutes. Roll out one piece of dough into an 8-inch (20-cm) circle. Place ½ cup (125 mL) pesto on half of circle, spreading to within ½-inch (1-cm) of edge. Moisten edge with water, fold over and seal edge with a fork. Prick dough in several places. Repeat with remaining dough and filling. Brush tops with one tablespoon (15 mL) oil.

Place on lightly greased baking sheet and bake at 400 F (200 C) for 15 to 20 minutes or until golden brown and baked. Remove from oven and brush with remaining one tablespoon (15 mL) oil. Serve with green salad. ★

PESTO IMPOSTORS

Pesto is traditionally made with basil. But the word itself means only "crushed." Cooks first made pesto by crushing the herb – along with olive oil, garlic, pine nuts and parmesan – in a mortar and pestle.

Today's cooks are more likely to use a food processor, and will play with a variety of herbs. If you're game to experiment, parsley, cilantro, spinach and even broccoli can stand in for the basil with surprisingly good results.

Italian Basil Loaf

Makes two loaves

In somewhere close to 90 minutes, you can pull a light loaf, saturated with basil flavor, out of the oven. This bread cries out for home-made soup.

5 cups (1.25 L) all-purpose flour, divided
2 (8-g) packages instant yeast
½ cup (125 mL) grated parmesan cheese
½ teaspoon (2 mL) salt
1¼ cups (300 mL) water
⅓ cup (75 mL) olive oil
3 tablespoons (45 mL) dried basil
2 large eggs, beaten

In large bowl, combine four cups (1 L) flour, yeast, parmesan cheese and salt. In small saucepan, heat water and oil until very warm, 125 to 130 F (50 to 55 C); stir in basil.

Stir warm water mixture into flour mixture. Add eggs and stir batter vigorously, until well mixed. Gradually add enough of the remaining one cup (250 mL) flour to make a soft dough.

Turn dough out on to floured surface and knead for eight to 10 minutes or until smooth and elastic, adding additional flour as needed. Cover and let rest 10 minutes.

Divide dough in half. Form each half into a round loaf. Cut an X about ¼-inch (5-mm) deep in centre of each loaf and place on greased baking sheets. Lightly dust loaves with flour. Cover and let rise until double in size, about 30 to 40 minutes.

Bake at 375 F (190 C) for 25 to 30 minutes or until loaves sound hollow when tapped on bottom. Cool loaves on wire rack. ★

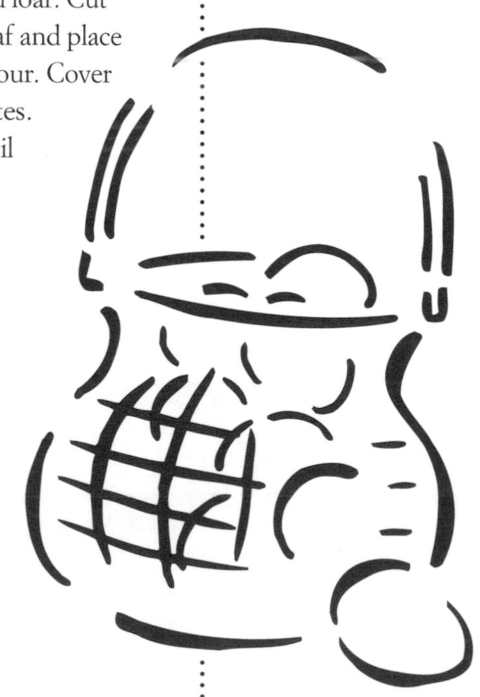

Focaccia with Sage Leaves

Makes two small loaves

The idea for this bread, with its charming decoration of three whole sage leaves baked into the top of each loaf, comes from The Greens Cookbook. But we wanted to pat our sage leaves into a faster dough, so we used instant yeast, and cut the rising time to 10 minutes. If you like to talk to your dinner guests as you finish cooking, playing with this bread is a pleasant last-minute chore. It's cooked by the time you get everything to the table and everyone seated.

2½ cups (625 mL) all-purpose flour, divided
1 (8-g) package instant yeast
1 teaspoon (5 mL) salt
¼ cup (50 mL) chopped fresh sage
1 cup (250 mL) water
3 tablespoons (45 mL) olive oil
½ teaspoon (2 mL) sugar
6 fresh sage leaves
Olive oil
Coarse salt

In large bowl, combine 1½ cups (375 mL) all-purpose flour, yeast, one teaspoon (5 mL) salt and chopped sage. In small saucepan, heat water, three tablespoons (45 mL) olive oil and sugar until very warm, about 125 to 130 F (50 to 55 C); stir into the flour mixture. Stir in enough of the remaining one cup (250 mL) flour to make a soft dough.

Turn dough out on to floured surface and knead for five minutes. Cover and let rest 10 minutes.

Divide dough in half. Roll or press each piece into a small oval, about ½-inch (1-cm) thick. Place on greased baking sheet. Make indentations on surface of dough with fingertips.

Press three sage leaves on surface of each oval, brush with olive oil and sprinkle lightly with coarse salt. Cover and let rise in warm place until double in bulk, about 20 minutes.

Bake in the top third of oven, at 450 F (230 C) for 10 to 12 minutes, or until done, spraying bread with a fine mist of water twice during first 10 minutes of baking. Serve hot. ★

RISING CONFUSION

Fast Rising. Rapidmix. Instant yeast. Who has a hope of keeping them straight?

Ever since manufacturers improved on traditional active dry yeast, home bakers have been reeling from the task of distinguishing Fast Rising yeast, which has to be proofed first by dissolving it in water, from Rapidmix, which can be added directly to dry ingredients.

Neither one is the same as Instant yeast, which can be mixed in with the dry ingredients, but demands that the wet ingredients be brought to a higher temperature than either of the other two yeasts.

Our advice: make sure the name on the yeast package matches the name specified in the recipe. And check carefully that your wet ingredients are the right temperature for the yeast.

PASTA FOR ANY OCCASION

On evenings when you free-wheel it in the kitchen, making a sauce while the pasta boils, using whatever the fridge offers, recipes are beside the point. Pasta is just part of a cook's vocabulary, like potatoes were to an earlier generation.

But if you want a spectacularly quick and wholesome dinner that tastes great, look here. We also have two company-dinner pastas, a homely baked ziti and a fabulous pasta salad – enough to round out your repertoire.

Virtuous Spaghettini Primavera

Makes four servings

It's quick. It's low-fat. It's creamy, studded with broccoli flowers and shiny strips of carrot, red pepper and snow peas. It feeds you enough grain and vegetables to make a modern nutritionist smile. All this and it tastes good too. Use a whole-milk yogurt in this recipe: the added fat is minimal.

½ pound (250 g) spaghettini
⅓ cup (75 mL) chicken or vegetable stock
2 garlic cloves, chopped fine
1 carrot, julienned
2 cups (500 mL) broccoli flowerets
1 red bell pepper, julienned
1 green bell pepper, julienned
1 cup (250 mL) halved snow peas
1 small zucchini, julienned
1½ cups (375 mL) plain balkan-style (thick) yogurt
Salt and freshly ground pepper to taste
Grated parmesan cheese

Cook pasta in large amount of boiling salted water until tender; drain.

In saucepan, heat stock. Add garlic, carrot, broccoli, red and green peppers, snow peas and zucchini. Cover and steam four to five minutes; drain.

Toss hot pasta with vegetable mixture, then with yogurt. Season with salt and pepper. Serve with parmesan cheese. ★

PASTA TIMING

How do you tell when your dried spaghetti is done? Forget throwing it at the ceiling. Instead, cut one of the noodles in half and look for a solid white dot at the centre. The minute that dot disappears, the pasta's cooked.

Fettuccine with Prawns, Red Pepper and Pine Nuts

Makes six servings

Everyone needs at least one good pasta dish for company. This is one of the best we've ever found. Prawns, red peppers and pine nuts, stir-fried with garlic, meet a buttery wine-and-shallot sauce when tossed into cooked fettuccine.

1 pound (500 g) raw prawn tails
2 cups (500 mL) dry white wine
½ cup (125 mL) finely chopped shallots
2 tablespoons (30 mL) chilled butter or margarine
Salt and freshly ground pepper to taste
½ pound (250 g) fettuccine
3 tablespoons (45 mL) olive oil
½ cup (125 mL) pine nuts, toasted
1 large garlic clove, crushed
2 large red bell peppers, seeded and julienned
2 tablespoons (30 mL) finely chopped fresh basil
1 tablespoon (15 mL) finely chopped fresh oregano

Shell, devein (see page 89) and butterfly prawns; set aside.

In saucepan, combine wine and shallots and bring to a boil over high heat. Boil until reduced to ⅔ cup (150 mL). Reduce heat to low and whisk in butter. Remove pan from heat if bubbles appear on surface. Season with salt and pepper. Keep sauce warm over hot water until ready to serve.

Cook fettuccine in large amount of boiling salted water until tender. While pasta is cooking, heat olive oil in large frypan over medium heat. Add prawns, nuts and garlic; saute two minutes. Add peppers; saute until peppers are tender and prawns are opaque, about two minutes.

Drain pasta and transfer to platter or bowl. Spoon sauce and prawn mixture over pasta and gently toss. Sprinkle with basil and oregano. ★

Penne with Spicy Sausage, Oyster Mushrooms, Basil and Tomatoes

Makes four servings

This is a fresh and sophisticated reworking of pasta with tomato sauce. Hot Italian sausage, oyster mushrooms and basil are the flavors that make it extraordinary. The recipe comes from Saltimbocca restaurant chef-and-owner, Ken Bogas, who came to the kitchen and cooked with us. One thing we learned: be sure to blanch the sausage well, then have the oil very hot or the sausage will fall apart.

4 hot Italian sausages
1 (796-mL) can Italian tomatoes, undrained
4 tablespoons (60 mL) virgin olive oil, divided
½ cup (125 mL) coarsely chopped fresh basil (loosely packed)
1 small onion, chopped
4 large garlic cloves, chopped fine
2 tablespoons (30 mL) finely grated carrots
Salt and freshly ground pepper to taste
2 cups (500 mL) sliced oyster mushrooms
¾ pound (350 g) penne pasta (about 5 cups or 1.25 L)
Grated parmesan cheese

Simmer sausages in water for about five minutes or until just cooked; let cool. Coarsely chop tomatoes in food processor.

In large frypan, heat two tablespoons (30 mL) olive oil. Add basil, onion, garlic and carrots; saute until soft. Season with salt and pepper. Add tomatoes and simmer for about 30 minutes.

Cut sausages diagonally into thin slices. In small frypan, saute sausages in remaining two tablespoons (30 mL) olive oil until lightly browned. Add mushrooms and saute until tender. Add mushrooms and sausages to tomato sauce; simmer five minutes.

Cook pasta in large amount of boiling salted water until tender; drain and return to saucepan. Add sauce and toss. Serve topped with parmesan cheese. ★

BASIL BONUS

If you grow your own basil, you can cut what you need. If you buy fresh basil by the bag, most recipes leave you with a lot of leftovers.

The best way to keep it: freeze it. Strip the leaves from the stems and put them in a mini-food processor or blender. Turn on the blender and add just enough olive oil to make a paste – about one tablespoon of olive oil to a cup of basil leaves. Freeze the paste in a small freezer bag and use it the next time you need basil to flavor a pasta sauce or a vegetable saute. The basil's green turns to black in the freezer, but the taste remains.

★ ★ ★ ★ ★

Baked Ziti with Eggplant and Ricotta Cheese

Makes six servings

This is a "Look, Ma, no meat" pasta dish: layers of pasta, eggplant cooked in tomato sauce and cheese. Ziti, by the way, is a tubular pasta a little like long macaroni. If you can't find it, use penne.

1 eggplant (about 1 pound or 500 g), peeled and cut into ½-inch (1-cm) cubes
Salt
1 pound (500 g) ziti
2 tablespoons (30 mL) butter or margarine
1 medium onion, chopped
1 garlic clove, chopped fine
¼ cup (50 mL) vegetable oil
1 (796-mL) can tomatoes, cut and undrained
1 (156-mL) can tomato paste
1 teaspoon (4 mL) salt, divided
1½ tablespoons (22 mL) chopped fresh basil
1½ teaspoons (7 mL) chopped fresh oregano
¼ teaspoon (1 mL) crushed dried hot red pepper
¼ cup (50 mL) freshly grated parmesan cheese
1 (500-g) container ricotta cheese
1 egg, beaten
3 cups (750 mL) grated mozzarella cheese

Place eggplant cubes in colander, sprinkle generously with salt. Let stand for 30 minutes. Rinse and drain thoroughly.

Cook ziti in large amount of boiling salted water until tender; drain. Add butter and toss to coat.

In large frypan, cook eggplant, onion and garlic in oil until tender. Stir in tomatoes and tomato paste, ½ teaspoon (2 mL) salt, basil, oregano and crushed red pepper. Bring to a boil. Reduce heat and simmer 15 minutes, stirring occasionally. Remove from heat and stir in parmesan cheese.

In small bowl, blend ricotta cheese, egg and remaining ½ teaspoon (2 mL) salt.

In shallow three-quart (3-L) casserole, layer half each: cooked pasta, tomato mixture, ricotta cheese mixture and mozzarella cheese. Repeat layering with remaining ingredients. Bake at 350 F (180 C) for 45 minutes or until cheese melts. ★

Orzo Salad with Snow Peas and Asparagus

Makes eight servings

Orzo is a small fine pasta that looks like rice when it's uncooked and like, well, orzo, when it's cooked. It's splendid with fresh dill and asparagus, as in this recipe given to us by Lazy Gourmet Susan Mendelson. When asparagus isn't in season, fresh green beans are a more than adequate understudy. This is, by the way, a great a picnic salad.

Salad:

- **2 cups (500 mL) orzo**
- **3 cups (750 mL) snow peas**
- **½ pound (250 g) asparagus**
- **1 tablespoon (15 mL) chopped fresh dill**
- **2 green onions, cut in small pieces**

Vinaigrette:

- **⅓ cup (75 mL) lemon juice**
- **2 garlic cloves**
- **1½ teaspoons (7 mL) Dijon mustard**
- **½ teaspoon (2 mL) salt**
- **¼ teaspoon (1 mL) pepper**
- **⅔ cup (150 mL) vegetable oil**

For salad: Cook orzo in large amount of boiling salted water until tender, about eight to 10 minutes; drain and chill.

Blanch snow peas in boiling water for 30 seconds; drain and chill immediately in cold water. Cut into bite-size pieces. Blanch asparagus in boiling water for one minute; drain and chill immediately in cold water. Cut into bite-size pieces.

In large bowl, combine orzo, snow peas, asparagus, dill and green onions.

For vinaigrette: Place lemon juice, garlic, mustard, salt and pepper in blender; process until well mixed. With blender running, gradually add oil.

Add vinaigrette to orzo mixture and toss. Cover and refrigerate until well chilled. ★

THREE WAYS TO COOK CHICKEN PRONTO

Boneless chicken breasts cook fast, and their mildness is an invitation for tomatoes and basil, garlic and balsamic vinegar to have their way with the taste of dinner. Besides, almost everyone likes chicken.

Get out the trusty frypan, pour a glass of wine for the cook and relax. Dinner's ready in less than half an hour.

Clockwatcher Chicken Cacciatore

Makes four servings

If you find yourself looking for quick dinners that children will like, pause here. You can get this meal on the table in half an hour – and for 15 minutes of that time the chicken cooks unattended while you take care of other dinner details. Two things make it widely popular: its mild flavor and the fact that spaghetti's involved.

2 tablespoons (30 mL) vegetable oil
2 whole chicken breasts, boned, skinned and halved
1 medium onion, sliced
1 (796-mL) can Italian-spice stewed tomatoes
1 cup (250 mL) dry white wine or chicken stock
1 teaspoon (5 mL) dried basil
¼ teaspoon (1 mL) pepper
½ pound (250 g) spaghetti, broken in half
¼ cup (50 mL) grated parmesan cheese

In large frypan, heat oil over medium heat. Add chicken and onion; brown chicken on both sides.

Add tomatoes, wine, basil and pepper to chicken; bring to a boil. Stir in spaghetti. Cover and simmer over low heat, stirring occasionally, about 15 minutes or until spaghetti is tender. Sprinkle with cheese, cover and cook for an additional minute. ★

CANNED SHORTCUTS

Most often, we're in favor of cooking from scratch. Still, some canned conveniences are worth using.

Italian-spice stewed tomatoes already have onions, celery, green pepper, basil and parsley in the can, ready to add flavor in a hurry.

If you have regular stewed tomatoes on hand you can, of course, go ahead and make Clockwatcher Chicken Cacciatore. Add more basil and some chopped parsley. It won't be exactly the same, but it will still be good.

Chicken Breasts with Balsamic Vinegar

Makes four servings

Some recipes are infinitely variable. We made this one – for chicken breasts simply cooked and served with a shallot, herb and balsamic vinegar sauce made from the pan juices – with marjoram. But it cries out for a test drive with basil, too, and tarragon, and, in the fall, some thyme. Of course, if you have oregano growing in your garden, that might be nice too...

- **2 whole chicken breasts, boned and halved**
- **Salt and freshly ground pepper**
- **2 tablespoons (30 mL) butter or margarine, divided**
- **1 tablespoon (15 mL) vegetable oil**
- **1 tablespoon (15 mL) finely chopped shallots**
- **3 tablespoons (45 mL) balsamic vinegar**
- **1½ cups (375 mL) chicken stock**
- **2 teaspoons (10 mL) finely chopped fresh marjoram**

Sprinkle chicken with salt and pepper.

Heat one tablespoon (15 mL) butter and oil in large frypan over high heat. Add chicken, skin-side down, and cook until skin is crisp. Reduce heat to medium-low; turn chicken breasts over and cook until chicken is done, about 12 minutes. Transfer chicken to heated platter and keep warm in oven.

Pour off all but one tablespoon (15 mL) fat from frypan. Add shallots and cook over medium-low heat for three minutes or until translucent, scraping up any browned bits. Add vinegar and bring to a boil. Boil for three minutes or until reduced to a glaze, stirring constantly. Add stock and boil until reduced to ½ cup (125 mL), stirring occasionally. Season to taste with pepper.

Remove sauce from heat and whisk in remaining one tablespoon (15 mL) butter and marjoram. Whisk in any juices from chicken. Spoon sauce over chicken and serve immediately. ★

BALSAMIC BASICS

Traditional balsamic vinegar is made from the cooked juice of grapes, aged for a minimum of 12 years in wooden casks, inspected and sanctioned by an official board of tasters and sold only in quantities of 3.3 ounces or less, at prices of well over $100 a bottle.

What you buy for $10 or so in Italian delis is an aged wine vinegar fortified with caramelized sugar, herbs and other flavorings, meant to satisfy the demand for traditional balsamic vinegar.

The affordable modern version may not be the elixir that was once presented to kings and emperors as coronation gifts, but it's still a wonderful tasting vinegar. Once you've tried it, you'll be tempted to add its rich, slightly sweet, slightly sour taste to a multitude of dishes.

★ ★ ★ ★ ★

GROW YOUR OWN TARRAGON

The hardest part of growing tarragon is getting the right plant.

French tarragon, the one with the bittersweet licorice flavor, looks almost exactly like Russian tarragon, which tastes like bitter grass. Bite before you buy.

Tarragon is a perennial that likes lots of sun and a moderately rich, well-drained soil. When your tarragon gets straggly, cut it to within two inches of the ground; it will bound back.

Parmesan Breaded Chicken Breasts with Lemon-Tarragon Sauce

Makes four servings

The easiest way to add instant luxury to dinner is, regrettably, to add fat. This recipe for chicken coated in bread crumbs and parmesan cheese, and topped with a buttery lemon-tarragon sauce, does, indeed, indulge in the pleasures of butter – but only to the tune of a tablespoon per person. Use it when you need something fabulous in a hurry.

2 whole chicken breasts, boned, skinned and halved
Salt and freshly ground pepper to taste
2 tablespoons (30 mL) flour
1 large egg, beaten
2 tablespoons (30 mL) water
1 cup (250 mL) fine fresh bread crumbs
¼ cup (50 mL) freshly grated parmesan cheese
2 tablespoons (30 mL) vegetable oil
¼ cup (50 mL) butter or margarine
1 tablespoon (15 mL) finely chopped fresh tarragon
2 tablespoons (30 mL) fresh lemon juice

Season chicken with salt and pepper. Coat with flour.

In shallow dish, combine egg and water. Combine bread crumbs and parmesan cheese. Dip floured chicken breasts in egg mixture, then in bread crumb mixture to coat thoroughly.

Heat oil in large frypan; add chicken and cook over medium-high heat for five minutes on each side or until golden brown and cooked through. Transfer chicken to a warm platter, discarding any excess fat. Add butter to frypan and cook until bubbling. Add tarragon and lemon juice; bring to a boil, stirring constantly. Pour over chicken breasts and serve. ★

★ ★ ★ ★ ★

Two Easy Ways with Fish Fillets

A filleted fish is as accommodating a kitchen partner as a breast of chicken. It doesn't really matter whether you use cod, halibut or snapper fillets in these recipes. Just be sure that the fish you buy gleams with freshness and smells clean, not fishy. Never accept anything less.

Broiled Cod with Balsamic Vinegar

Makes four servings

Sometimes the simplest things are best. All you do here is broil cod fillets and top them with a sauce made from butter, oil, balsamic vinegar and sun-dried tomatoes. I'd want to have some plain pasta to eat with this fish, the pasta dressed with nothing more complicated than a little olive oil and a light grating of parmesan and freshly ground pepper.

- 1½ **pounds (750 g) cod fillets**
- **Salt and freshly ground pepper to taste**
- 2 **tablespoons (30 mL) butter or margarine**
- 1 **tablespoon (15 mL) vegetable oil**
- 1½ **teaspoons (7 mL) balsamic vinegar**
- 1 **tablespoon (15 mL) finely chopped sun-dried tomatoes (packed in oil)**
- 1 **tablespoon (15 mL) chopped fresh parsley**

Broil cod about five minutes or until cooked. Season with salt and pepper.

In small saucepan, melt butter with oil over low heat. Add vinegar and sun-dried tomatoes; cook until heated through, about one minute. Remove from heat and stir in parsley. Spoon over cod and serve. ★

Onion-and-Zucchini-Smothered Snapper Fillets

Makes four servings

This recipe is best made in the summer, when tomatoes and basil are at their peak. But even without vine-ripened tomatoes, it's still a lovely, gentle supper of fish and vegetables. When you can't buy good fresh tomatoes, good-quality canned tomatoes are a better substitute than mushy, pink mid-winter imports. And try using cod or halibut instead of snapper. It's equally good.

1½ pounds (750 g) snapper fillets
3 tablespoons (45 mL) butter or margarine
1 onion, sliced thin
1 small zucchini, julienned
1 tablespoon (15 mL) chopped fresh basil
½ teaspoon (2 mL) salt
¼ teaspoon (1 mL) pepper
2 small tomatoes, seeded and chopped
2 tablespoons (30 mL) grated parmesan cheese

Arrange snapper in greased shallow baking dish just large enough to hold fish in single layer.

In small frypan, melt butter. Add onion and saute just until soft, separating into rings as they cook. With slotted spoon, remove onion rings and spread over snapper. Stir-fry zucchini in same frypan until slightly soft; spoon over onions. Combine basil, salt, pepper and tomatoes; spoon over zucchini. Sprinkle with parmesan cheese.

Cover loosely with foil and bake at 450 F (230 C) for 12 minutes per inch (2.5 cm) thickness or until fish flakes when tested with a fork.

To serve, remove vegetable-topped fish with slotted lifter and serve immediately. ★

CHOCOLATE

I ate two pounds of Valrhona chocolate while writing this book. Mostly I ate chunks of it, by itself or with fruit. Sometimes I cut it small and ate it on bread and butter. This is a guilty habit of mine, although I feel much less guilty if it's a good whole-wheat bread. Open-faced chocolate sandwiches: they'll catch on one day, honest.

In my sordid chocolate habits I am a true representative of the test kitchen. Barbara McQuade is a chocoholic who can be lured into debauchery by a well-timed truffle. And it's always a pleasant moment in the kitchen when we find a particularly good chocolate recipe and Brenda Thompson points out that it's going to have to be tested again – in metric. (With baking, particularly, you can't just punch in the conversions.)

We do try to restrain ourselves. Nevertheless, we can't help having a very good collection of chocolate recipes. These recipes are arranged in order of their culinary age, from the most childlike to the most sophisticated.

Dirt Pie

Makes eight servings

Turn to this recipe when you've decided to have some nutritionally incorrect fun with the kids. Ask yourself: what do they need more? Another rice cake or memories of making something gooey, bad, easy and fun?

The entertainment value comes from gummy worms writhing on top of the chocolate filling, with chocolate cookie crumbs masquerading as dirt. You'll find gummy worms in most candy stores. Just don't put them on top of the pie until the last moment. They'll seize up in the fridge.

Crumb Crust:

1¼ cups (300 mL) graham cracker crumbs
¼ cup (50 mL) sugar
¼ cup (50 mL) butter or margarine, at room temperature

Filling:

6 cups (1.5 L) chocolate ice cream
20 chocolate sandwich cookies (Oreos, etc.)
1 cup (250 mL) miniature marshmallows
Gummy worms for decoration

For crust: Combine crumbs, sugar and butter; mix well. Press mixture over bottom and sides of 9-inch (23-cm) pie plate. Chill in refrigerator while making filling.

For filling: Let ice cream soften slightly in the refrigerator to a creamy consistency. Meanwhile, coarsely grind cookies in food processor (or chop with knife).

Measure ice cream into bowl and work with wooden spoon until soft enough to fold in miniature marshmallows and 1¾ cups (425 mL) of the cookie crumbs (reserve remaining crumbs).

Spoon mixture into pie shell and sprinkle top with remaining cookie crumbs. Cover with plastic wrap and freeze until firm, about four hours.

To serve, remove from freezer and decorate with gummy worms. Let stand in refrigerator about 15 minutes before slicing. ★

TAKING THE ICE OUT

How impatient are we? Someone in the test kitchen uses the microwave to soften premium ice cream when it first comes out of the freezer. Why stand around waiting when gratification can be instant?

You don't need much time or much power, and microwaves vary, so start slow, say 20 seconds at medium power, until you find the optimum power and temperature for your oven.

★ ★ ★ ★ ★

Chocolate Peanut Marble Brownies

Makes 20 brownies

A whirly, swirly brownie. Peanut butter takes over where chocolate leaves off. Your instincts might be to use the best peanut butter you can get. Restrain yourself. What this recipe needs is a creamy, kid-style commercial peanut butter. The all-natural, no-additives kind makes a brownie that's too dry and dense.

- **6 (1-ounce) squares semi-sweet chocolate**
- **2 tablespoons (30 mL) butter or margarine**
- **½ cup (125 mL) creamy peanut butter**
- **¼ cup (50 mL) vegetable oil**
- **2 cups (500 mL) packed brown sugar**
- **4 large eggs**
- **2 teaspoons (10 mL) vanilla**
- **1½ cups (375 mL) all-purpose flour**
- **½ teaspoon (2 mL) salt**
- **1½ cups (375 mL) coarsely chopped unsalted peanuts**

In small saucepan, melt chocolate and butter over low heat; stir to blend and set aside.

In medium bowl, beat together peanut butter and oil. Beat in sugar. Beat in eggs, one at a time, beating well after each addition. Beat in vanilla. Beat in flour and salt just until combined.

In small bowl, stir together one-third of the peanut butter batter and the cooled chocolate mixture. Stir peanuts into remaining peanut butter batter.

Spread peanut butter batter evenly in greased 13x9-inch (33x23-cm) baking pan. Spoon chocolate mixture over batter. With knife, make a zigzag through the layers to create a marbled effect.

Bake at 325 F (160 C) for about 30 minutes or until outer edges are baked (centre may still be slightly soft). Cool brownies in pan set on wire rack. Cut into pieces about 2½x2 inches (6x5 cm). ★

ZAP YOUR SUGAR

It's dispiriting to reach for the brown sugar and find a lump as hard as concrete, especially if you're all set to do some baking.

Put a mug full of water and the sugar, in its bag but with the bag open, in the microwave. Microwave on high for 30 seconds, let it stand a minute, then check to see if it's soft enough. If it isn't, give it another 30 seconds.

Lean Chocolate Sheet Cake

Makes 25 servings

The interesting thing about this recipe is not that it has half the fat content of our older, more traditional chocolate sheet cake (7.41 grams of fat per serving instead of 16). The interesting thing is that when we offered the old and the new side by side in a blind tasting, most people liked the low-fat cake better and assumed that it was the "bad" one. This recipe makes lots: it's a good cake for a crowd.

Cake:

- **2 cups (500 mL) all-purpose flour**
- **1⅔ cups (400 mL) sugar**
- **½ cup (125 mL) unsweetened cocoa powder, sifted**
- **1 cup (250 mL) water**
- **½ cup (125 mL) vegetable oil**
- **1 cup (250 mL) buttermilk**
- **1 large egg, beaten**
- **2 teaspoons (10 mL) baking soda**
- **1 teaspoon (5 mL) vanilla**

Frosting:

- **3 tablespoons (45 mL) butter or margarine**
- **3 tablespoons (45 mL) unsweetened cocoa powder, sifted**
- **1 teaspoon (5 mL) vanilla**
- **3 cups (750 mL) icing sugar**
- **4 tablespoons (60 mL) buttermilk**

For cake: In large bowl, combine flour, sugar and cocoa; set aside. Combine water and oil in saucepan and heat until mixture comes to a boil; stir into flour mixture.

Mix together buttermilk, egg, baking soda and vanilla. Add to flour mixture; stir until well combined. Spread batter in greased 15x10-inch (38x25.5-cm) jelly roll pan.

Bake at 350 F (180 C) for 18 to 22 minutes or until done. Let cool in pan on wire rack.

For frosting: In large saucepan, melt butter. Remove from heat and stir in cocoa and vanilla. Alternately blend in icing sugar and buttermilk until frosting is smooth. Spread on top of cake. Cut into 3x2-inch (7x5-cm) pieces. ★

DUTCH TREAT

The first European hot chocolate drinks were made from sweetened bars of chocolate, grated and melted in hot wine. Hot milk came a little later, and so did cocoa.

The first person to press so much fat out of the cocoa bean that only a powder remained was Conrad Van Houten, who began to manufacture cocoa for drinking in 1828.

Van Houten was also the first to treat drinking chocolate with an alkali solution. The process, called "Dutching," darkens the color, reduces the natural acidity and mellows the flavor.

The words "Dutch Process" are no guarantee of quality. In cocoa, as in coffee, quality begins with the bean.

Pecan Fudge Sheet Cake

Makes 25 servings

Perhaps our files bulge with good sheet cake recipes because Pat Pederson has four children. Sheet cakes are a mother's easy out: they're quick and make lots of servings. If you're not so concerned about fat, and you want nuts with your chocolate, try this one.

Cake:

- **1¾ cups (425 mL) all-purpose flour**
- **1½ cups (375 mL) sugar**
- **½ cup (125 mL) unsweetened cocoa powder, sifted**
- **2 teaspoons (10 mL) baking powder**
- **½ teaspoon (2 mL) salt**
- **1 cup (250 mL) milk**
- **¾ cup (175 mL) butter or margarine, at room temperature**
- **4 large eggs**
- **1 teaspoon (5 mL) vanilla**

Cocoa Pecan Frosting:

- **½ cup (125 mL) butter or margarine**
- **¼ cup (50 mL) unsweetened cocoa powder, sifted**
- **6 tablespoons (90 mL) milk**
- **1 teaspoon (5 mL) vanilla**
- **3½ cups (875 mL) icing sugar**
- **1½ cups (375 mL) chopped pecans**

For cake: In large bowl, combine flour, sugar, cocoa, baking powder and salt. Add milk, butter, eggs and vanilla; blend ingredients together on low speed of mixer. Beat at medium speed for one minute.

Pour batter into greased 15x10-inch (38x25.5-cm) jelly roll pan and spread evenly. Bake at 350 F (180 C) for 35 to 45 minutes or until done. Top with frosting while cake is still warm.

For frosting: In medium saucepan, melt butter. Remove from heat; stir in cocoa. Blend in milk and vanilla alternately with icing sugar until smooth. Stir in nuts. Pour frosting over warm cake and spread evenly over top. Let cool until frosting is set. Cut into 3x2-inch (7x5-cm) pieces. ★

Chocolate Bar Chocolate Chip Cookies

Makes about four dozen cookies

I'd never want to lay claim to the ultimate chocolate chip cookie. After all, what's "ultimate" to one chocolate lover is either pitifully weak or grossly overdone to another. But if your ideal chocolate chip cookie is on the soft and chewy side, and you like the idea of intensifying the effect of the chocolate chips by adding a grated milk-chocolate bar, try this recipe.

1 cup (250 mL) butter or margarine, at room temperature
1 cup (250 mL) granulated sugar
1 cup (250 mL) packed brown sugar
2 large eggs
1 teaspoon (5 mL) vanilla
2 cups (500 mL) all-purpose flour
2½ cups (625 mL) quick-cooking oats
½ teaspoon (2 mL) salt
1 teaspoon (5 mL) baking powder
1 teaspoon (5 mL) baking soda
2 cups (500 mL) semi-sweet chocolate chips
1 (100-g) bar milk chocolate, grated
1½ cups (375 mL) chopped nuts

In large bowl, cream together butter and both sugars. Beat in eggs and vanilla.

In separate bowl, combine flour, oats, salt, baking powder and baking soda. Process in blender, in small amounts, until flour mixture forms a powder.

Add flour mixture to butter mixture, a third at a time, until just blended. Add chocolate chips, grated chocolate and chopped nuts.

Using two level tablespoons (30 mL) dough for each cookie, shape dough into balls. Place 2 inches (5 cm) apart on ungreased baking sheet. Bake at 375 F (190 C) for about 14 minutes. ★

Chocolate-Pepper Hearts

Makes about four dozen cookies

Deeply, darkly chocolate with a bite of pepper, these cookies are the most satisfying way I've found to end a spicy meal. Serve them with ice cream, or with fresh mangoes; either way the sweet-spicy reminder of the heat of the main course is immensely satisfying.

- **1½ cups (375 mL) all-purpose flour**
- **¾ cup (175 mL) unsweetened cocoa powder, sifted**
- **¾ teaspoon (4 mL) ground cinnamon**
- **¼ teaspoon (1 mL) salt**
- **⅛ teaspoon (0.5 mL) finely ground black pepper**
- **Generous pinch cayenne pepper**
- **¾ cup (175 mL) unsalted butter, at room temperature**
- **1 cup (250 mL) sugar**
- **1½ teaspoons (7 mL) vanilla**
- **1 large egg**

Combine flour, cocoa, cinnamon, salt, black pepper and cayenne pepper; set aside.

In large bowl, cream butter. Beat in sugar and vanilla, then egg. Stir in flour mixture. Shape dough into a disc; wrap in foil or plastic wrap and chill until firm, about one hour.

Place dough on lightly floured surface or between two sheets of wax paper and roll to ⅛-inch (2.5 mm) thickness. Cut out hearts with a 2½-inch (6-cm) cookie cutter. Place on lightly greased baking sheet.

Bake at 375 F (190 C) for five to six minutes or until set. Place cookies on wire rack to cool. ★

UNSWEETENED CHOCOLATE

Is unadulterated chocolate with no sugar, lecithin, or vanilla. It's pure chocolate liquor – the thick, dark-brown paste left when cocoa nibs are roasted and ground to extract some of the cocoa butter. Also called bitter or baking chocolate.

BITTERSWEET CHOCOLATE

Has sugar, lecithin and vanilla added to the basic chocolate. Bittersweet chocolate usually has a higher percentage of chocolate liquor – and therefore a more intense chocolate flavor – than semi-sweet chocolate.

SEMI-SWEET CHOCOLATE

Has sugar, lecithin and vanilla added to the basic chocolate. Is likely to be sweeter and less intensely chocolate than bittersweet, but the two can be used interchangeably in cooking.

WHITE CHOCOLATE

Just a smooth sensation masquerading under the name of chocolate. A mixture of sugar, cocoa butter, milk solids, lecithin and vanilla, white chocolate contains no chocolate liquor.

CHOCOLATE CHIPS

Have been specially formulated to hold their shape when heated. Don't try to substitute chocolate chips for melted semi-sweet chocolate; they're much too thick when melted.

Sour Cream Chocolate Cake with Chocolate Frosting

Makes 12 servings

This simple, one-layer chocolate cake is feather-light but delivers an intense chocolate flavor. It's attractive too, especially if you go the whole nine yards and add the optional eight ounces of white and dark chocolate curls in diagonal lines across the top. For the most satisfying flavor, use European bittersweet chocolate.

- **4 (1-ounce) squares unsweetened chocolate**
- **2½ cups (625 mL) sifted cake flour**
- **2 teaspoons (10 mL) baking soda**
- **½ teaspoon (2 mL) salt**
- **½ cup (125 mL) butter or margarine, at room temperature**
- **2¼ cups (550 mL) packed brown sugar**
- **3 large eggs**
- **1½ teaspoons (7 mL) vanilla**
- **1 cup (250 mL) dairy sour cream**
- **1 cup (250 mL) boiling water**
- **4 (1-ounce) squares semi-sweet chocolate for garnish, optional**
- **4 (1-ounce) squares white chocolate for garnish, optional**
- **Chocolate frosting (see next recipe)**

Grease and flour 13x9-inch (33x23-cm) baking pan. Line bottom with wax paper; set aside.

Melt unsweetened chocolate in top of double boiler over hot (not boiling) water; set aside to cool. Combine flour, baking soda and salt; set aside.

In large bowl, cream butter. Gradually beat in brown sugar. Add eggs, one at a time, beating well after each addition. Beat in vanilla and melted chocolate. Alternately blend in flour mixture and sour cream, a third at a time, on low speed of mixer. Add boiling water; blend well.

Pour batter into prepared pan. Bake at 350 F (180 C) for 35 to 40 minutes or until done. Cool cake in pan for 10 minutes, then remove to wire rack to cool completely.

While cake is cooling, cut curls from semi-sweet and white chocolate (don't mix the dark and white chocolate curls).

Ice cooled cake with chocolate frosting and immediately cover the top of cake with the dark chocolate curls. Then, place five (1-inch or 2.5-cm) strips of wax paper at approximately 1-inch (2.5-cm) intervals diagonally on top of semi-sweet curls. Sprinkle white chocolate curls over areas between the paper strips. Remove paper strips. Cut into pieces about 3x3 inches (7x7 cm).★

Chocolate Frosting

- **¼ cup (50 mL) butter or margarine**
- **4 (1-ounce) squares unsweetened chocolate**
- **3½ cups (825 mL) sifted icing sugar**
- **½ cup (125 mL) milk**
- **1 teaspoon (5 mL) vanilla**

Melt butter and chocolate in top of double boiler over hot (not boiling) water. Place in bowl and cool to lukewarm. Add icing sugar, milk and vanilla. Mix on low speed of electric mixer for one minute or until smooth. Chill until of spreading consistency, about five minutes. ★

HOW TO MAKE CHOCOLATE CURL

Take the chill off your chocolate before starting; if it's too cold, the chocolate will be brittle and will splinter instead of curling. Leave it for several hours in a warm place – on top of the refrigerator, for example – or give it five seconds in the microwave on medium power.

Make the curls with a vegetable peeler, drawing it carefully across the smooth surfaces of the chocolate.

Use a toothpick to lift the curls without breaking them.

Almond Bark Brownies

Makes 20 brownies

Almond bark brownies might just fulfill your requirements for the perfect brownie. The almonds give more texture than walnuts, and a much stronger, nuttier taste. Like the Chocolate Peanut Marble Brownies, (page 137) these bake in a 13x9-inch pan, which is more than most brownie recipes make. We think it's best to err on the safe side. After all, somebody might drop by.

Batter:

- **1⅓ cups (300 mL) all-purpose flour**
- **1 teaspoon (5 mL) baking powder**
- **½ teaspoon (2 mL) salt**
- **1 cup (250 mL) butter or margarine**
- **1 cup (250 mL) unsweetened cocoa powder, sifted**
- **2 cups (500 mL) sugar**
- **4 large eggs**
- **1½ teaspoons (7 mL) vanilla**
- **1½ cups (375 mL) unblanched whole almonds, toasted**

Chocolate Glaze:

- **½ cup (125 mL) butter or margarine**
- **¼ cup (50 mL) unsweetened cocoa powder, sifted**
- **½ teaspoon (2 mL) vanilla**
- **2 cups (500 mL) icing sugar**
- **¼ cup (50 mL) milk**

For batter: In small bowl, combine flour, baking powder and salt; set aside.

In large saucepan, melt butter. Remove from heat and stir in cocoa, followed by the sugar, eggs and vanilla. Stir in flour mixture.

Spread batter evenly in greased 13x9-inch (33x23-cm) baking pan. Sprinkle almonds evenly over surface. Bake at 350 F (180 C) for 25 to 30 minutes or until done. Cool in pan.

For glaze: In medium saucepan, melt butter. Remove from heat. Stir in cocoa and vanilla. Alternately blend in icing sugar and milk until glaze is smooth and of pouring consistency. Pour chocolate glaze over brownies. Chill until glaze is set. Cut into pieces about 2½x2 inches (6x5 cm). ★

Double Chocolate Pecan Pate

Makes 16 servings

Served with raspberry puree, chocolate pate can look intimidatingly difficult. But keep in mind that all you're really doing is melting the chocolate, stirring in some other ingredients and letting the chocolate solidify again in a new shape: piece of cake. The particularly happy combination of added ingredients in this recipe comes from Mary Mackay, then chef at the Frog and Peach restaurant, now baker at Terra Breads. Belgian chocolate gives the best results, but it's expensive – use as much of it as your budget will allow and make up the rest with less expensive baking chocolate.

1 pound (450 g) semi-sweet chocolate
1½ cups (375 mL) whipping cream
½ cup (125 mL) unsalted butter
1½ cups (375 mL) pecan halves, toasted
1 tablespoon (15 mL) grated orange rind
1½ teaspoons (7 mL) orange-flavored liqueur
½ teaspoon (2 mL) vanilla
½ teaspoon (2 mL) ground cinnamon
2½ cups (625 mL) fresh raspberries, about
Sugar to taste
Whipped cream for garnish
Raspberries for garnish
Mint sprigs for garnish

Line bottom and sides of 8x4-inch (20x10-cm) loaf pan with plastic wrap.

Finely chop chocolate and place in large bowl. In saucepan, scald cream and butter. Pour over chocolate and stir until chocolate is melted. Stir in pecans, rind, liqueur, vanilla and cinnamon.

Pour chocolate mixture into loaf pan. Let cool, then cover and chill in refrigerator for three hours or overnight. Invert pan and unmould on to platter. Peel off plastic wrap.

Puree raspberries in blender or food processor; press through sieve to remove seeds. You will need one cup (250 mL) puree. Sweeten to taste with sugar.

With warm sharp knife, cut chocolate pate into about ½-inch (1-cm) slices. To serve, pour one tablespoon (about 15 mL) raspberry puree on each dish. Place chocolate slice on dish and garnish with whipped cream, raspberries and mint. ★

Iced Almond Roca Cappuccino Squares

Makes about 18 servings

Assembled desserts are guilty pleasures. For one thing, they bring to mind visions of vanilla pudding mixes and rainbow mini-marshmallows. Our guidelines: don't use anything you wouldn't be happy to eat all by itself; and, you can't go too far wrong if you start with premium ice cream. We found this combination of coffee ice cream and chocolate wafers in the Good Housekeeping Illustrated Book Of Desserts, and played around with it. The almond roca candy was our idea.

1 (200-g) package chocolate wafers, crushed
½ cup (125 mL) butter or margarine, melted
2 litres coffee ice cream
1 tablespoon (15 mL) coffee-flavored liqueur
1½ cups (375 mL) crushed almond roca candy (about ½ pound or 250 g)
Semi-sweet chocolate curls for garnish

Mix crushed chocolate wafers and butter in 13x9-inch (33x23-cm) baking pan. Reserve ½ cup (125 mL) chocolate wafer mixture; press remainder evenly over bottom of pan. Chill in refrigerator while preparing filling.

Remove coffee ice cream from containers and put in large bowl. Place in refrigerator for about 20 minutes to soften slightly, stirring occasionally.

Stir ice cream until smooth, adding liqueur. Spread half the softened ice cream over the wafer crust. Top with crushed candy and reserved crumb mixture, pressing lightly.

Spread remaining ice cream over top. Cover and freeze until firm, at least four hours.

To serve, let dessert stand at room temperature about 10 minutes for easier cutting. Cut into squares. Garnish with chocolate curls. ★

Chocolate-Dipped Cappuccino Shortbread

Makes about 34 cookies

Although I cannot for the life of me figure out what's so Christmassy about chocolate-and-coffee shortbread, the truth is I bake these cookies during the Christmas holidays and at no other time. Given how rich they are, and how irresistible (cold, out of the fridge, with the chocolate bits ready to fragment in your mouth just in advance of the rich, coffee-flavored shortbread), that's probably just as well.

Caterer Jane Bailey of Candlelight Cuisine in Ocean Park gave us the recipe for a story on gifts from the kitchen. If you can bear to give them away, pack these treats into a handsome tin or a gift mug.

4 teaspoons (20 mL) instant coffee
1 cup (250 mL) butter, at room temperature
½ cup (125 mL) sugar
½ teaspoon (2 mL) vanilla
1¾ cups (425 mL) all-purpose flour
¼ cup (50 mL) cornstarch
6 (1-ounce) squares semi-sweet chocolate, melted

Finely crush instant coffee in coffee grinder. In large bowl, cream together butter and sugar. Beat in instant coffee and vanilla.

Sift flour and cornstarch together; stir into butter mixture. Mould into the shape of coffee beans, using one tablespoon (15 mL)of dough for each cookie. Using the back of a knife, press an indent about ⅛-inch (2.5-mm) deep, lengthwise, across the top of each cookie. Place on greased baking sheet.

Bake at 325 F (160 C) for 15 minutes. Place on wire racks to cool.

Dip both ends of cookies in chocolate. Place on baking sheet lined with wax paper and refrigerate. ★

CHOCOLATE MELT-DOWN

It used to be that melting chocolate without burning it demanded a double boiler. The rule was: Over, not in, hot, but not boiling, water.

Microwave ovens have made the chocoholic's life much easier.

To melt two ounces of chocolate, put the chocolate in a bowl and turn the microwave on to medium power for two to three minutes. If you're melting a larger quantity, it will take longer.

Don't be tempted to turn the heat up. At higher temperatures, you're much more likely to burn the chocolate.

And don't think the chocolate hasn't melted just because it's still standing in a block. Stir it first before heating it longer.

Gundel Crepes with Rum, Raisins and Walnuts

Makes 12 servings

Gundel palacsinta are crepes made as they were in Budapest's famous Gundel restaurant. They showed up in our kitchen the day chef Michael Pinter came in to cook a Hungarian dinner. This is a serious, show-stopping dessert: crepes stuffed with a rum-infused walnut-and-raisin filling, swimming in a powerful bittersweet chocolate sauce.

One word of warning for those who don't always read recipes right through before starting to cook: the raisins in the filling need at least 12 hours to soak in the rum.

Crepes:

- 4 large eggs
- 2⅓ cups (575 mL) cold milk
- ¾ cup (175 mL) icing sugar
- Pinch salt
- 2⅓ cups (575 mL) all-purpose flour
- 2 tablespoons (30 mL) soda water
- Vegetable oil

Filling:

- ⅔ cup (150 mL) raisins
- ⅔ cup (150 mL) dark rum
- 4 cups (1 L) walnut pieces
- ¾ cup (175 mL) whipping cream
- ¼ vanilla bean
- 2½ cups (625 mL) icing sugar
- 1 teaspoon (5 mL) grated orange rind

Chocolate Sauce:

- 6 large egg yolks
- 2 cups (500 mL) icing sugar
- ½ cup (125 mL) unsweetened cocoa powder
- 1 cup (250 mL) milk
- 1 cup (250 mL) whipping cream
- ¼ vanilla bean
- 7 (1-ounce) squares semi-sweet chocolate
- Rum

POD POWER

No European ever tasted vanilla before Hernando Cortez brought it back to the Spanish court. Like chocolate, it's a new-world flavor.

You get the sweetest, most fragrant and purest vanilla flavor from vanilla beans, the seed pods of the vanilla plant. Look for them in specialty and spice shops, where they're sold in plastic tubes.

Vanilla beans are expensive. Get the most out of them by using them more than once.

After you've used part of your vanilla bean in the filling and sauce for these crepes, save the pieces and let them dry for several days.

Then place the dried beans in a jar of sugar and seal it. The sugar will take on a delicate vanilla aroma.

For crepes: Place eggs in bowl. Add milk, icing sugar and salt; whisk until smooth. Gradually whisk in flour until smooth. Stir in soda water.

Heat a 6- to 7-inch (15- to 17.5-cm) crepe pan over medium-high heat; add about one teaspoon (5 mL) oil and heat.

Pour about three tablespoons (45 mL) batter into pan, quickly tilting and rotating pan to spread batter thinly and evenly. Continue tilting and rotating until batter stops running.

When bottom is lightly browned and top almost dry, about 30 seconds, turn crepe. Cook just enough to dry bottom side, about 15 seconds. If batter seems too thick, thin with a little soda water. (Batter should be about the consistency of whipping cream.) Repeat with remaining batter. Makes about 24 crepes.

For filling: Soak raisins in rum overnight. Drain and reserve rum for sauce.

Finely chop walnuts in food processor. In saucepan, scald cream with vanilla bean; discard vanilla bean. In bowl, combine walnuts, icing sugar and orange rind; add hot cream and stir to mix. Stir in raisins and set aside.

For chocolate sauce: Place egg yolks in bowl and set aside. Sift icing sugar and cocoa together; gradually beat into egg yolks.

In saucepan, scald milk and cream with vanilla bean; discard vanilla bean. Gradually whisk scalded mixture into egg yolk mixture.

Melt chocolate in top of double boiler over hot (not boiling) water. Gradually whisk in egg yolk mixture; cook until sauce thickens, stirring constantly. Measure reserved rum and add extra, if necessary, to make ½ cup (125 mL); stir into sauce.

Spread each crepe with about three tablespoons (45 mL) of filling and fold in half. For each serving, place two crepes on plate and top with some of the chocolate sauce. ★

★ ★ ★ ★ ★

INDEX

(Boldface type denotes recipe by its full name)

A NOTE ON HERBS

Many of the recipes in this book call for fresh herbs. If you need to substitute dried herbs, use less. Drying usually concentrates flavor. Start with one part dried to replace three parts fresh, then adjust to suit your taste.

★ ★ ★ ★ ★

D

E

F

G

T

U

V

W

Y

Z